Trapped in Paradise:
A Memoir

Cindy Art

Please note while this is a non-fictional story, some names have been changed to protect the privacy of those involved. This book includes opinion on the subject matter.

DEDICATION

This book is dedicated to those whom have been affected by the Troubled Teen Industry, and struggling families.

CONTENTS

ACKNOWLEDGMENTS

Special thanks to those whom helped with this project. I am sincerely grateful for your assistance and support.

Edited by Ramona Marten. Cover Art by Francyne Williams.

i

1 - WORKSHEETS

'Every morning I would sweep and dust the room impeccably. And every morning after the staff did their rounds I would receive a 'warning,' a demerit, because I had supposedly missed dusting off a spider web. This meant the staff noted my cleaning chore as unsatisfactory which gave me a demerit and put me one step closer towards getting me into worksheets.'

Because of a spider I was in worksheets often when I first arrived. I sat on a hard chair facing the wall, in a roughly two-foot cubby desk made of plywood. The walls of the room were white, with a cold dark floor. The room was narrow, and was in the shape of an 'L.' Cubbies were lined up next to one another in rows against the wall. There were no windows, and it was humid and stuffy. Sometimes there was a fan, but it did little, if anything to cool or remove the hot air. I'd sit there for hours, silent, not allowed to 'avert my eyes' from the test I was being given and expected to pass. Passing the test wasn't a problem. After a while, I remembered all the answers to the tests; the 'worksheets.' There were lots of 'students' that also had been there and done that. The staff was on to them. Eventually, they made a rule that one was not allowed to complete the answers ahead of time. One had to listen to the tape and fill out the answers as they came up on the tape. I listened for hours to the monotone cassette tapes echo through the desolate room as they played. I circled my answers with what was left of a crayon. Students in worksheets weren't to be trusted with a pen or pencil because they might try to hurt someone.

Someone in worksheets was expected to pass so many tests before being allowed to rejoin their group. One worksheet test was given for each tape. The number of passed worksheets needed to be released depended on the severity of the rule violation. The punishment was meant to give one time to reflect on their misbehavior. I learned early on that the system was unjust and corrupt. I was silently resentful.

Upon arriving to Jamaica I was assigned a morning job, as was everyone else who resided there as a student. The first job I was assigned was sweeping the room I slept in, and dusting off the shutters. Every morning I would sweep and dust the room impeccably. And every morning after the staff did their rounds I would receive a 'warning,' a demerit, because I had supposedly missed dusting off a spider web. This meant the staff noted my cleaning chore as unsatisfactory which gave me a demerit and put me one step closer towards getting me into worksheets.

There was a spider that lived on the shutters of my room. Every morning I would dust off its web, and every morning before chore inspections it would rebuild its web just in time to get me into trouble. It wasn't as though I had a choice of coming back to destroy its home at a later time. I was to follow a strict schedule, and was not allowed to leave the group I was assigned to.

Each morning after inspections the staff would read off who had received an inspection violation demerit. Following, the students who had received a total of three demerits for the week would be taken from the group and sent into worksheets. I had tried to explain my situation, but it didn't seem to make a difference. I was laughed at by the staff member who had done the inspections. Who would really believe a kid sent away for being a troublemaker anyway? A story about how a spider would magically rebuild its web just after I cleaned off its home. It was some kind of speedy stealth spider. I suppose it really did sound like an excuse, but I was actually telling the truth. And every three days I would be sent to worksheets because of it. I would receive one demerit per day for each violation. Then I'd be off to worksheets to think about what I had done.

At one point, I got my group staff Ms. Henney to care. A few staff seemed to care about the kids in the beginning. Ms. Henney decided to look at my cleaning job personally right after I had completed it. And one time, she even helped me. After completing my cleaning job, I was off with my group for the day. Usually, there was fitness, and then breakfast. Sometime shortly after those the cleaning violations would be read. And sure enough, that day, the spider had rebuilt its web and I had received a warning. Ms. Henney fought for me with the other staff member, yelling in patois, and reneged my demerit. It was a major victory.

I remember when I first arrived to Jamaica. I stepped off the plane to immediately notice the humidity. I felt as though I couldn't breathe the air was so thick. I then wandered through customs and found myself outside the airport. I didn't know who was coming to pick me up, or who I was looking for. I found my way back inside and asked someone in a uniform if he knew of anyone who was supposed to meet me. He answered in patois, and I had no idea what he said to me because I couldn't understand his accent. Eventually, I was coordinated with the driver. He escorted me to a van. During our drive I looked outside the window and saw the beauty of the beach, along with all the colorful buildings and shacks. The island was gorgeous. It was so green and the ocean so blue. The sun was shining, the weather was warm and I strangely felt relaxed. I started to think because I was in such a beautiful place, maybe I really would change my ways. I thought I might learn to deal with my shortcomings.

We drove for about half an hour and the driver pulled over to make a rest stop. He asked if I wanted to get out, but I decided to stay in the van. He brought me back a soda. I did not realize that would be the last soda I would have in a very long time. I would have savored it more had I known. After the stop we drove for another hour or two. The driver was clearly familiar with the narrow road. Speeding around corners, beeping as he went to warn the other drivers zipping by at high speeds, I began to wonder if I ought to start praying that I would make it out of that van in one piece. On my way to the facility I saw lush vegetation and beautiful mountains. It's a shame that was essentially the last I saw of the island until I was driven back for my return flight to the United States, 18 months later.

I arrived at the facility. It was a white building with a white fence in the front. It was a converted hotel, right on the beach. There were two large gazebos on the far right of the property, and coconut trees on the left side in the yard; picture perfect from the outside. It was surrounded by lush green mountains, bright blue sky and sand. I found out years later the picture of the outside of the building was in the marketing materials my father had seen. It was however, the only actual thing that wasn't fictional in the contents of the materials. The other contents included photos of kids in regular clothes, sitting on actual couches in furnished rooms with colorful painted walls where framed pictures hung. They showed kids doing things like playing the guitar or studying in actual classrooms with desks.

The description WWASP gave of their program to parents described a friendly island convenient because of its proximity to services available in the United States. Students were described as being able to benefit from a cultural experience. They describe 'TASK' seminars used for emotional growth. There is mention of a supposedly appropriate educational curriculum with students in a classroom environment tutored by a teacher. The description the WWASP program gave to parents described students daily personal development and emotional growth courses. It discusses offering an appropriate balance of recreation and social activity in their schedule.

In my opinion, this was all a farce. I had no real experience of the island. I learned nothing about the island history or culture. Many people found the seminars emotionally abusive, because people were verbally attacked after being forced to share very personal aspects of themselves. The facilitators were relentless and unreal in the amount of fear they used amongst the kids, and pushed the kids emotionally to their limits. There was one seminar facilitator in particular who was known for calling a majority of the teenage girls sluts. He would try to get them to state if they were 'on the outs' they would sleep with him. As an adult, it is pretty obvious now he did that to inflate his own ego. He took advantage of an emotionally vulnerable situation. It is simply despicable. The seminars brought people into the room from breaks to the sound track from 2001 Space Odyssey. Attendees needed to be back in

4

their chairs by the time the music ended or faced confrontational feedback in front of the group about how being late to their seat was a 'reflection of their life.' The seminars got people to do strange things like dress up in costumes and perform in front of the group. More than anything, I felt as though I had to cry 'enough' when sharing so that I wouldn't be given feedback about not opening up or dealing with my 'issues.' At the end of the seminars, those who made it through and were not kicked out (or 'chose out' as the program would like to say) made a list of exhausting goals.

The education in the program was a joke. Many of their courses were not accepted into the educational system in the United States, where a majority of the students were from. I can't recall any personal development or emotional growth course offered. There was not an appropriate balance of recreation and social activity, as all of the time was scheduled for most students and social interaction was very tightly regulated. The picture painted in the marketing materials was far from what I experienced in the program.

2 - A RUDE AWAKENING

'Back at home I was a rather rebellious kid with magenta hair, ripped up jeans, some sort of band t-shirt, and excessive costume necklaces. I wore blue nail polish and an exorbitant amount of dark eye makeup. Here I was, in Jamaica, in a sundress.'

Upon arriving at the facility I spent my first few hours with a tall thin woman named Ms. Dacey, who was my case manager. I could hardly understand her through her thick accent. She was to inventory my belongings. They were packed by my father and grandmother in a large green plastic tub, which is the way I later learned, is how everyone else had their belongings stored. The coordination and conformity of 'The Program' and the parents was astounding I shortly learned. It must have taken a lot of effort to get it all together. I had no idea I was being sent away to a foreign land. Apparently, neither did my mother, whom I was living with at the time. It was entirely my Father and his Mother's doing.

My belongings were inventoried in the room I was to be staying in. Each room had several bunk beds, each perfectly made. All had sheets and no blankets. I got a glimpse of worksheets upon my entrance to the dorms, as it was at the end of the hall. The monotone tape was playing and there were several girls sitting on the floor in the hall, looking me over. Ms. Dacey talked to me, but I had little understanding of what she said. She spoke in English, but her accent was Jamaican Patois. I became overwhelmed and started to cry. I thought I would be comforted in some manner, but I was basically told to suck it up.

Ms. Dacey pulled out a sundress from the green bin my father sent and instructed me to put it on with a t-shirt underneath. I objected, but I had no other option. I put on a white spaghetti stringed sundress with bright colored flowers on it. It was the complete opposite of what I would be wearing had it been my choice.

Back at home I was a rather rebellious kid with magenta hair, ripped up jeans, some sort of band t-shirt, and excessive costume necklaces. I wore blue nail polish and an exorbitant amount of dark eye makeup. Here I was, in Jamaica, in a sundress. I was told what was packed for me was what I was to wear until my uniforms arrived.

I was given a handbook of all the rules I was to follow. It must have been at least a quarter inch thick. I was instructed to read it, carry it with me, and study it at night.

It became time for me to be put with the other girls and into the routine of the program. When I arrived, most of the other girls were in worksheets. Right before I arrived there had been some sort of mass 'statement of facts' confession, used as a group wide punishment, so only one or two girls were out of worksheets doing the regular daily schedule. I was assigned a senior student, to help me learn the rules over the next few days.

I met the first few girls who were out of worksheets. When I arrived it was fitness time in the front yard. I was so overwhelmed, confused, exhausted, and sad. The last thing in the world I felt like doing was exercise. I tried not doing it, but was firmly instructed by staff to follow the routine the other girls were doing. Together, the girls were mimicking an exercise video one of them had remembered from when they were at home in the United States. They moved together in harmony, in their uniforms, which they had hiked up into their undergarments to allow extra air to circulate. Exercise in hot humid weather is horrid. And I am one of the least coordinated people I know. I had a hard time following the whole routine, and I got sunburned. Fitness time ended. I hadn't yet learned anything substantial about my peers other than they appeared very compliant. They gathered together and took a look at me. After figuring out how I fit in terms of stature, all the girls lined up in height order heel to toe, and counted off for the staff 'headcount.' This was the first of many lines I was to walk in and headcounts I was to count off in over the next two years. The staff filled out their paperwork, radioed in the headcount and we set off for dinner.

We went to the dining hall, which was only semi-enclosed from the outdoors, and consisted of round white plastic patio tables, and white plastic chairs. The dining hall was in the center of the facility, constructed mainly from different types of cinder blocks, and painted white with the bottom portion of the room painted mustard yellow. We lined up to get our meal from the kitchen, which was passed to us over a cement counter. I remember I initially had problems with the staff because they tried feeding me meals with meat and I was a vegetarian.

Boy was I lucky to be a vegetarian. As though the food wasn't bad enough, having things like boiled cabbage for breakfast and then lunch, the carnivores were forced to eat things like boiled fish with the eyeballs still in, chicken foot soup, ox tail, and curried goat. Often, when curried goat was being served, one less goat would be seen in the yard outside the facility.

After dinner we had music time in a circle around an open patch underneath a group of trees. Music time consisted of girls singing. We had no instruments, tape players or karaoke machines like the marketing materials my father received had suggested. Of course, I hadn't known that was what he was told because I had no idea I was being sent away. I had never seen the brochures or the video.

When music time was over, there was an educational video we were to watch, and a 'reflections' sheet to fill out, which consisted of a set of questions to answer daily on a sheet of paper asking how one felt, what was accomplished during the day, and goals for the next day. It was turned in at the end of each day and given to the case manager.

At the end of the day my assigned senior student showed me how to make my bed properly. I got to see a lot of faces pile in to the dorms that I had not yet met. However, none of them were allowed to talk to me. They had been put on 'silence' because they were still in trouble; they hadn't completed all their worksheets. Not that they were allowed to talk to me without permission anyway because it was against the rules.

Letters from home were passed out at night in the dorms. The silence made for a good time to read letters, write to family, and journal. I remember the time before 'shut-down' (when it was bed time) was my favorite time of the day. I had some peace and quiet, and was able to unwind a little. I got to rest until the morning. In the mornings I would be abruptly awoken to a Jamaican woman yelling up and down the hallway '6:30 ladies. Time to wake up. Line up for head count.'

3 – GROUNDHOG DAY

'That is what just about every day looked like. Wash, rinse, repeat.'

Being in Jamaica was hard. I was put in a uniform similar to those of girls in Jamaican public schools. I was stripped of everything I could identify with. I was not free to talk without permission, or sit or stand without asking to do so. I was constantly watched and was never alone. The only thing I had to myself were my own thoughts. Time for my own private thinking eventually became impeded upon as the program director changed the daily routine to include monotone 'motivational' tapes to be played at all meals, of which I would be tested on later in the day as to how the taped lecture could improve my life.

Each day was the same. The students were assigned to permanent groups whom they spent all of their waking and sleeping moments with. Each group had a schedule that was strictly adhered to. There was 'reading' where the same *Chicken Soup for the Soul* book was read over and over again until the pages fell out.

Other activities included 'Music' where there were no teachers, instruments, radio or music player. The students sang songs that were approved of in advance, some of which became so commonly heard I thought my ears might bleed. Despite this, singing became something I learned to enjoy.

'Fitness' was done twice a day for half an hour each time, and 'P.E.' was done once a day for an hour. Both were the same. There was no reason to name them any differently. No teachers, no sports equipment of any kind, and typically no fun. At one point my father had some sports balls sent over. The different groups played with them so much they became flat. And they even played with them flat because there was no other option. A lot of that time was spent walking around the field in circles.

'School' was done six days a week. There was no formal instruction. I was assigned books to read from my grade level and was expected to pass a test for each chapter with a grade letter of 'B' or higher. Most of the time I just stared at the book blankly, wrote in my notebook, and fantasized about going home. I day dreamed about all the things I wished I could do like wear my own clothes, use a washing machine, cross my legs, wear make-up, eat the foods I missed, watch TV and just about any other freedom I wasn't allowed in Jamaica.

'Meal Time' was supposed to have half an hour to eat, but it often was only 10 or 15 minutes. Meals typically consisted of a plate half full with rice, and some other food, like oily cabbage and soggy bread. Other typical items included some sort of boiled green matter, lima beans, or chewy dumplings. The food wasn't exactly authentic, and was hardly palatable, yet all students were forced to eat at least half. I found the food so intolerable that I would usually just eat my half in rice. As the program grew in size and had more students, the portions of food became smaller and smaller. I lost so much weight while I was there my hip bones jutted out. My face was sunk in.

'Group' consisted of sitting in a circle made of plastic lawn chairs with our case manager present. The idea was to share something personal and explain supposed progress. I avoided sharing if I could, but it was inevitable. If I didn't share voluntarily, I would be called on to do so. I would stand up in front of everyone and divulge some nugget from my life that made it seem like I was learning from the program. Then the circle of group members would give feedback. There was even the chance of being given feedback if one didn't share. Either way, the feedback usually entailed how one 'wasn't working the program' or how one was a bad kid. Every time one would find him or herself on the defensive, one would then have to listen to the other students say not to justify behavior. Doing so was considered making an excuse. Often, one student would give feedback followed by another until the entire group had given feedback. The feedback was rarely constructive; it was demeaning and emotionally abusive. One had to give feedback to one's own friends. Ultimately, it was better not to take it personally because there was no other choice.

The end of the day had an 'Educational Video' followed by 'Reflections.' The selection of educational videos was limited. The entire collection was eventually watched over and over again. After viewing a video students were expected to write their thoughts down on how the information on the video improved their lives onto a 'Reflections Sheet'. The reflections sheet consisted of things learned that day, improvement on oneself, how one felt that day, how one achieved their goals for that day, and goals for the next day. It might have actually been useful to set goals had time been given to pursue them.

And there you have it. That is what just about every day looked like. Wash, rinse, repeat. The only difference in the schedule was on Sundays. There was a 'major cleaning' duty assigned to each group and there was no school that day. The group was given time for 'leisure and recreation,' which wasn't something we got at any other time during the week. This consisted of sitting in a room and socializing for about an hour. People would play games, write home, and sometimes staff dictated what to do in 'leisure and recreation' time.

I, like everyone else, had everything stripped away that resembled who I was. I wore a uniform, I was forced to wear my hair up, I wasn't allowed pluck my eyebrows or wear make-up. I was away from my family, I was away from my friends, the food wasn't familiar, and my surroundings inside the facility in Jamaica were depressing. The facilities had tile floors and wood shutters instead of windows. The beds were murphy style and folded into the wall; made out of unfinished wood and metal pipes. The chairs were all plastic. The table tops were made out of plywood covered in fake leather and were constantly sticky. The plumbing was unreliable and often feces would pile up in toilets for days, forcing those who wanted to wash their hands or clean themselves to use the hose outside on the basement level; even for bathing. The bottom of the pool; which was hardly used; was covered in a layer of thick bumpy brown crud. Laundry was all done by hand out of a bucket.

The program used fear tactics. Punishment for even minor infractions was severe. Students were not allowed to have a say in anything. Objection was a serious offence, punished with verbal abuse called feedback, or demerits, worksheets, observation placement where one laid on the floor for days, weeks or months, physical restraint followed by physical pain, or a combination of all those things. This oppression, followed by the living conditions broke down its captives.

The goal of the program was to break down the will of the student by giving them no other choice but to comply and adopt their ways. It was hopeless. I can find no other way of describing the program other than it being like a cult. The program tactics fit the definition of the word 'cult' precisely.

It was easy for the administrators of the program to get a hold of the minds of the students, seeming they were children and under their control. Somehow though, the program got a hold of the parents. Many parents got together in scheduled group meetings in or near their home towns. In my opinion, this was to make the parents feel better about sending their child away. Together, they convinced themselves they did the right thing. Many firmly believed their children would have surely died had they not been sent to the program. They risked everything to keep them there. My father paid $80 a day to keep me there. Some parents gave up their homes in order to afford the expense. Parents affirmed one another that anything negative the students said about the program was simply a manipulative tactic.

'April 28th, 1998

The staff is not letting us have the 'leisure time' our parents think we get. The group is being forced to sit in silence. The staff pulls so much crap that no one 'outside' knows about. And then my family wonders why I don't like it here and am unhappy. I guess I've never really made it clear, because I am afraid of getting into trouble. I feel so violated and disrespected as a person. Every day I feel as if I am being punished. I am barely even allowed to talk most of the time.'

On Sundays a movie would play on the television and snacks were given. Sweet snacks were only given on Sundays. Options included bag juice (a big sugary ice-pop) and Ovaltine biscuits. Some weeks the staff didn't get it together enough to have snacks, so I had to wait for weeks to taste something sweet. Usually the movie exceeded the amount of time allotted for 'movie time' and the video would be cut off without showing the ending.

4 - WORKING THE PROGRAM

'The whole system there was unjust. Nothing made sense.'

The program entailed earning merits. These were earned by complying with the rules. One had to earn a certain amount of merits before becoming eligible for a higher level. Each level had a set of privileges and consequences. There were six levels all together. Levels one through three did not differ much. The only significant difference was the amount of scheduled phone calls one got to make home under the watch of the assigned caseworker. Phone calls home began at level three. Getting the first three levels was easy. They were automatic after obtaining so many merits, as long as one didn't get demerits for rule violations, and laid low without getting some sort of group demerit.

Upper level kids were levels four, five and six. They had more freedom. They had the ability to set some of their own schedule, walk alone, spent some time by themselves, wear makeup and their own clothes, wear their hair down, could cross their legs, had more phone calls home, were allowed to listen to music, and were allowed to sit, stand and talk without permission, except when in class. In exchange they worked with the lower level students several days a week as staff members. Life was a lot better for them.

Obtaining levels four through six was more difficult. It required a vote up sheet, justifying why one deserved to be on such level, and required going in front of one's assigned group, teacher, case manager, group manager, the student council, and the facility administration. All mentioned required 'vote-up' approval before being able to move up to the next level. It required unanimous signatures on a vote up sheet.

Typically, all the required signatures were easy for me, except for the student council. The student council was a very small group of only upper level students when I first came into the program. It used to be honest and genuine. However, as it got larger, it consisted of cliques who broke the rules and engaged in scandalous behavior without the staff knowing. They were a group of girls who looked out for one another and had each other's backs. They didn't want to ruin a good thing, and wouldn't vote people up whom they thought might tell on them. Most lower level students followed the rules and were trying to better themselves. So, the vote up process to upper levels became problematic because the student council was corrupt.

The whole system there was unjust. Nothing made sense. The staff was not trained to work with children and often times disciplined the whole group for something they suspected one person in the group had done. Demerits were given for just about anything. It was a nightmare. I couldn't leave. And I couldn't communicate to my family what was going on. I was trapped in paradise.

I became very depressed. Despite being constantly surrounded by people, I felt alone, hopeless, and abandoned. After a while I thought about running away, making a break for it, and jumping off the roof of the building in hopes of killing myself, just so that I didn't have to repeat the same day over and over again. When I brought up how I was feeling in group, I was verbally attacked. I was often given feedback about how I wasn't 'working the program' which was then relayed to my father and grandmother. They would write to me about what a horrible child I supposedly was.

5 – A LITTLE BACKGROUND

'As an adult it continues to irritate me that my father singled me out as a misbehaving, uncooperative kid. It never occurred to my father to look at the environment he surrounded me in. He decided that I was the problem and sent me off to get fixed.'

My father is a compulsive hoarder. Compulsive hoarding stems from mental illness. It causes people afflicted to obsessively acquire seemingly useless objects in large quantities. Items are collected and often stored in piles in their homes, which impedes the flow of foot traffic inside to the point of having paths in one's home. Some hoarders have tendencies toward collecting certain types of items, like stuffed animals, dolls or cans for example. In the case of my father, objects of electrical or mechanical use are of particular interest to him. He worked as an engineer, and has a high intellect. To some degree, the items he saves feed that interest. He saves items such as half broken VCR's, old televisions, salvaged wiring components, nuts bolts and screws, and at one point had six faulty lawn mowers. He has long obsolete computers and computer software from the 1980's and 1990's. He has typically been a very introverted person, and enjoys reading. He hoards a large amount of books, most of which he has never read. Many are stored in paper bags. However, some items are clearly not to feed his engineering mind. In more recent years he has started to save product packaging and cereal boxes which he trims down to store knick-knacks in. He brings home used clothing without relation to size or necessity. He has obsolete children's toys in his home despite not having any young children in his life. He saves all papers and magazines. He keeps trade show schwag.

Hoarders are unable to bring themselves to part with objects. In the case of my father, the idea of moving or disposing of objects induces anxiety. In many instances, living conditions become what is considered uninhabitable. Dust, dirt and dander collect in the living space and affect air quality in the affected space. Many homes become fire hazards or are condemned. Sometimes animals or people can die in hoarder homes because of being buried under clutter that fell, or because rescue workers were not able to access a person in an emergency in a hoarder home. My father has worked in fire protection engineering for over twenty five years, so the fact that his home is a fire hazard is simply atrocious.

My father keeps his items in living space, in the attic, in the basement, in the garage, in the driveway, and in the front and back yard under tarps faded and tattered by sun, wind and rain. His hoarding even occurred at his job, where he was repeatedly written up for the lack of organization in his office.

Hoarders often have a distorted sense of reality in terms of the severity of their problem, much like those with addictive substance abuse problems. They fail to comprehend how their behavior affects their quality of life, and the lives of those around them.

Compulsive hoarding has been with my father for longer than my lifetime. He has put his hoarding first before his family, and has even become physically violent over it, thus my mother and father's divorce when I was twelve years old. My mother left *him*, not 'us' as he would like to believe.

My father was physically violent for years towards my mother and me. I remember him repeatedly punching me in the stomach and throwing me up against the wall one time for an accident that happened. And I remember waking up in the middle of the night to hear a crashing noise, with my mother crying who later slept in my room with me. In the morning she had bruises.

One day my father was upset about something that my mother had moved of his and he attempted to strangle her in front of me with a telephone cord. My mother suggested us sleeping in the car of the parking lot of a small shopping center after incidents like that. While his violence towards my mother ended with their divorce, it continued with me until he sent me to Jamaica. I think my mother should have left years before she did. Maybe she didn't leave because she hadn't had a job since I was very young, and didn't have the updated skills to find a good job to support herself. She stayed with a neighbor friend for a long time after leaving my father.

I, on the other hand, didn't have a choice to leave. I was stuck living with my father after the divorce. He obtained custody of me. My father and mother used the same lawyer for their divorce because my mother lacked the funds to obtain her own legal counsel. My mother had no one to counsel her or protect her best interests. My father benefited wholly from this situation because he was the one paying for the legal service. My mother, thinking it would be in my best interest, gave my father full custody of me. In her mind this meant I would live in a financially stable home and go to a better school than if I lived with her in Oakland. No one informed my mother of the concept of split custody.

Perhaps she was right in some ways. Living with my father in Livermore made it possible for me to attend much better schools. In the months prior to being sent to Jamaica, I lived with my mother in Oakland where I attended a public school. It was terrible. The kids were rough, fighting all the time at school, and at one point I was the victim of a threat from someone I didn't even know. That environment only escalated my pre-existing social anxiety. I reached a point where I was cutting classes and eventually stopped going to school entirely. Why neither of my parents recognized the cause of my cutting class beats the hell out of me.

Prior to that, I lived with my father in Livermore. I lived in a home piled from floor to ceiling with clutter and was expected to attend dinner at a table covered in papers, cereal boxes, and dusty old useless objects with just enough room to put a plate down. This is what my father expected me to appreciate and respect. My father and all his *things* were what I was supposed to want to be a part of.

I always felt like an odd kid growing up. I had internalized this oddness by the time I was a teenager, but looking back I realize I just felt different from the rest of my family. Everything was backwards with them. Their behavior frustrated me, and that is why I was such an angry child. As an adult it continues to irritate me that my father singled me out as a misbehaving, uncooperative kid. It never occurred to my father to look at the environment he surrounded me in. He decided that I was the problem and sent me off to get fixed.

My childhood was chaotic, but there were a few good memories. My relationship with my parents was good until I was old enough to know better. I helped my father around the house with his 'man-chores' such as painting, putting things together with nails, and working under cars with him. One time I helped him pull out the dent from my mother's car. He was so proud of his preschool aged daughter helping him work under cars he took a photo, and kept it in his wallet to show his friends and colleagues. He used to take me to the park all the time and climb to the top of the monkey bars with me on his shoulders. He taught me how to ride a bike. My father was my world during my preschool years.

I remember baking with my mother and going to Gymboree classes. I loved to sing in the car, and my mother would try to sing along with me. She would take me to the park and watch my friends over at our house for play dates. She read to me every night. She probably got me just about any toy I had ever wanted. We went on walks around our neighborhood in the Oakland hills, surrounded by trees. She always had some sort of art project for me. She made dinner every night; though I hesitate to call her a cook (I didn't know until I was in my early twenties that someone who wasn't a professional baker could make a cake that wasn't out of a box).

While there were good times, they were often overshadowed by the insurmountable clutter, the constant yelling between my parents, my father's scary piercing scream, the physical abuse, and my complete utter frustration with their behavior.

When I initially moved to Livermore with my father after the divorce of my parents, my father expected me to help him move everything he owned. He bought a trailer, probably about five feet by four feet, and hauled most of his possessions behind his Toyota Camry. When he wasn't using that, he used a truck he borrowed from a friend. Sometimes a son of his friend, Matthew, came over for the weekend to help with the move. Being that my father is a hoarder, the amount of items to move was inconceivable. By the time he was done moving, his four bedroom house with a three car garage, an attic, driveway, and our acreage of land were filled to the brim with junk and clutter.

Any twelve year old girl in a new town would want to spend the summer playing with the other neighborhood kids rather than help her father physically move his belongings into the house. The only thought I have as to why my father didn't hire a moving crew is because he was, and still is, too frugal to do so. He apparently thought a significant part of this responsibility of moving his enormous amount of belongings fell to me, as my being part of the family and doing my fair share included me hauling his many possessions up the two-flights of stairs from the basement of our family home in Oakland to his new home in Livermore. He is very attached to his belongings. My father saw and continues to see 'respecting' his clutter as part of respecting his home. This is a big reason why I was an angry child that wanted little to do with him.

My father's expectations have always been ridiculous. He moved into a new home with his twelve year old daughter and felt that I should be interested in all the things he deemed to be of interest for a girl my age, like cheerleading, horseback riding, and violin lessons. In elementary school I was a very talented violin player, but I lost interest when I started to feel the pressure of competing seriously. It then was no longer something fun that I wanted to continue. I just wanted to go out and play with the kids in the neighborhood. I suppose he tried though.

I don't recall my father and I going out of Livermore often. Most of the events we attended were related to his job and were never of cultural or artistic value. I don't recall him participating with me in activities that I enjoyed, like art. My father's interests are engineering and mechanics, which perhaps explains why he didn't have anything he was passionate about to share with me. He didn't know how to relate to people let alone a teenage daughter. Maybe he had expectations of what he wanted me to become or be interested in and became frustrated when I didn't fulfill his expectations (or in his words 'didn't cooperate'). I was the one who 'messed things up' and he held my mistakes against me, instead of looking at what he was doing as a parent. I was sent to Jamaica because, in his mind, I was the problem. It was as though he had no part in it and was not responsible for the situation.

When the major move ended, my father continued to have his friend's son Matthew stay for some weekends to help him with things around the house. I developed a major crush on him. He was rough around the edges. He smoked and would sneak around the block for a cigarette, avoiding smoking in front of my father. He was cute and I thought hanging out with him was awesome. Eventually I started going around the block with him and smoking. I had never smoked before, but I thought it was an excuse to spend time with him.

After moving to Livermore, I attended summer school. Not because I needed the credits but because my father wanted to keep me busy. In the fall I started school at one of the local middle schools. When I moved to Livermore I decided I no longer wanted to be known as my full name, so I shortened it to Cindy. I wanted a fresh start. I wanted to get away from being the awkward kid I was in elementary school. I started the school year with a group of new friends.

One of my new friends at school was named Feldon. We became close friends. He was a good kid and together we hung out with a group of other kids. Feldon didn't like my smoking. He would steal my cigarettes from me and toss them down the sewer. As my home life became more turbulent, I drifted away from that group of friends and found myself with a different crowd. Over the previous summer I had spent a lot of time with some kids in my neighborhood. Tom was one of them. He lived a couple blocks down from my house, and we became close friends.

My father deemed driving me to school as 'inconvenient' because it was in the opposite direction as his commute to work. He thought I should find my own way to school. So I walked or rode my bike to school with Tom. Hailey (another neighborhood kid), who lived on the block between Tom and I, would walk with us. On our way to school, Tom, Hailey and I would often smoke cigarettes and talk about the things in our home lives that we never talked about with anyone else.

Tom was adopted and lived in a house on College Street known to police as 'The College Street Crack House.' The people who lived there used drugs, but crack wasn't one of them. June, Tom's adopted mother, used to work as an engineer if I recall correctly, but had developed a number of health problems. Over the years she became addicted to pain killers and relied heavily on marijuana for relief. June was a kind woman who took people into her home whom otherwise had no other place to go. I felt safe at her house, and felt as though I belonged. I felt as if I was part of a family. June brought a lot of people into her home and under her wing. Because of her kindness, people called her Mom, including me.

There were drugs in that house. I smoked cigarettes and had my hands on marijuana from time to time. An older boy at June's house named Jake had an interest in me and I didn't discourage him. Somehow this was less chaotic and more emotionally supportive than my home environment.

Tom was a truly genuine person and I trusted him completely. He was like a brother to me and I felt safe with him. He was my best friend for a long time. Often in trouble with the law, he was on probation for several years. He once broke into a church to play hide and seek and got caught, he shoplifted, and once was caught setting a fire near a school. I got in trouble with him once for drinking in public. We were close friends, known by other kids close to our age, and had a large group of friends.

The situation at my father's house was bad. I was depressed and suicidal. I began writing suicide notes talking about my family frustrations, and feeling sad and misunderstood. At one point I took sleeping pills with a ton of aspirin in attempts to kill myself. I went to sleep not knowing if I would ever wake up. I woke up though. I lived another day to draft another suicide note, which my father found. I don't know how he found it, but my guess is that he rifled through my trash and discovered it. My father often went through the trash to protect anything he deemed valuable from being thrown away.

My father, the man who sifted through his daughter's trash to find items to save, sent me to the juvenile psychiatric ward for evaluation. After that I went to live with my mother in Oakland.

After moving back in with my Mother in Oakland, I spent a lot of time with Hailey. Hailey ran away from her home in Livermore because her grandparents abused her. She went to live with her friend Laura in the Oakland ghetto. I would often make way to the MacArthur BART station where Hailey and Laura would meet me. We would walk deep into the ghetto of Oakland where Hailey was living. Laura and Laura's mother took Hailey in when she ran away from her grandparents in Livermore. Laura's mother was a single mother, and could have used a lot of help. I remember there not being food in the house when we spent time there. Often we would all walk to the store to get ramen noodle soup from the package, or potatoes to make French fries. Once, Hailey got kicked out of a grocery store for stealing food (because she didn't have any money to eat).

For some reason, Hailey, Laura and I decided to all shave the bottom halves of our hair off. I think it may have started as a dare to shave all of Hailey's hair off. Hailey was the first, I was second, and Laura was the third. As I recall, the area she lived in was bad and riddled with gang wars. After we shaved our hair, we kept the top part down so the other people in the neighborhood wouldn't think our similar haircut was a gang symbol. In retrospect, being there was a bad situation. I'm lucky nothing bad happened to me while spending time there.

Eventually, Hailey spent time at my house because my mother didn't like where I was hanging out. I attended junior high down the street from my home in the prestigious Oakland Hills. I was a minority however, because students were bused in from rough parts of Oakland to attend what was considered a better school. Because of this, most of the local kids did not attend the local junior high. Parents who lived in my neighborhood sent their children to private school after elementary school. I asked to be sent to private school, but ended up at the local middle school when I went to live with my mother. I wasn't used to being one of the only caucasian people at school and it made me very anxious. It was a rough school. Because of this I stopped attending class and spent most of my time with Hailey instead. We smoked cigarettes and marijuana together and I enjoyed her company.

We hung out at my house sometimes, but more often we were at Laura's house. Occasionally, we would venture out of the house. One time we walked several blocks down to see someone Laura knew. We wound up going to the back of an abandoned apartment building where Laura's friend was hanging out. Her friend was smoking crack with some squatter who offered to share some of it with us. We declined.

While my mother has not always made the best decisions, she knew I was not hanging around the safest area, and asked Laura's mother not to let me leave the house when I came over to visit. I am glad now that she was looking out for me. She saved me from what turned out to be a horrible situation that happened to my friend Hailey.

The same night my mother made me promise to stay inside, my friend Hailey went to go get marijuana. The dealer wanted to 'hang out.' Apparently, he was at a hotel. He wanted Hailey and I to meet him there. Hailey said we did not have a way to get there and he sent a cab over. Laura's mother told me she had promised my mother she wouldn't let me go outside the apartment, so Hailey went by herself. Hailey came back several hours later and said he gave her marijuana, but supposedly she had been raped. To this day, I feel devastated for her yet incredibly relieved I wasn't there for it to happen to me. Why I decided to obey my mother's wishes that night I don't know, but I am more than grateful that I did. It was at that point in my life I was clearly headed in the wrong direction.

I was due for a visit with my father shortly after that. I remember the morning he came to pick me up. I didn't want to go. Something in my gut told me to stand my ground and stay home, but my mother told me I really ought to spend time with my father. My father arrived, and I reluctantly left with him. For our visit he brought along his girlfriend of the time, Callie, and we went to San Francisco. We spent time at Pier 39. They were awfully nice to me that day. They ate what I wanted to eat, and were overly kind. We actually went out and spent time together doing something interesting. I was suspicious.

That night I was in Livermore at my father's house. I asked to go spend time with Tom since I hadn't seen him for a while. My father let me, but emphasized that I had to be home on time. That was odd to me. I could be angry and defiant, but wasn't often late. I typically came home by curfew so his emphasis of being home on time struck me as strange.

Tom and I spent time with our friends that night. We went and smoked pot in a large tool shed we found open in our friend's apartment complex. As Tom and I walked home, we were pulled over by the police. They had their guns raised and asked us to put our hands up. Apparently, Tom matched the description of a kid who had stolen a gun. The police patted Tom down and questioned him on the side of the road. Realizing they had the wrong person, they let us go. I returned home startled and stoned, but on time. I went to my room. That was the beginning of what became a very bad turn of events for me.

6 - KIDNAPPED

'What a great thing it would have been to take off in that car. Being a fourteen year old girl at the time, I was worried about being in trouble with the police for stealing a car. But looking back, it might have gotten me out of that whole mess altogether.'

The date was April 14th, 1997; it was the night I received the knock at my bedroom door that changed my life forever. It was the night I was 'kidnapped' and began my journey to Jamaica. My nightmare began.

There was a knock on my bedroom door around 11:00 p.m. I was reading a magazine in bed. My father came into my room and told me there were some 'people he wanted me to meet.' I thought it was an odd request at such an hour, but I tried to be polite. A man and a woman entered my room. I shook their hands and was told they 'were going to get me some help.' I didn't put up a fight and went willingly. Despite this I was told by the man 'we could do this the easy way or we could do this the hard way, with handcuffs.' It was as though the man said it just to assert his authority and build up his ego. He grabbed me by my overalls rather abruptly, even though I was going willingly. Because he did so, they ripped on my way into his car. These people I later learned were professional kidnappers. The program had helped coordinate this transaction with my father for a fee. The children were later told to call them escorts, not kidnappers. This practice has since been made illegal in the state of California, where I was living at the time.

We drove for hours with me in the backseat of the car all through the night, until we reached Reno, Nevada. We pulled up to a dimly lit house. There the escorts picked up another child. A girl. Her name was Shari. We sat together in the backseat of the car. I was happy to have her company and glad to not be in it alone. They continued to drive through the night until it became light. They stopped to get gas. Then we drove for hours on a road through miles and miles of red dirt and shrubs through the desert until the driver was pulled over by the police for speeding. The cop literally appeared out of nowhere.

Upon pulling over, the man and the woman were asked to step out of the car by the police officer. The keys were left in the ignition. Shari and I looked at one another. Both of us knew exactly what the other was thinking. Should we steal the car and get away from these people? We both wanted to. I didn't really know how to drive though. And by the time we were done trying to figure out the logistics our escorts were back in the car. We had missed our chance.

What a great thing it would have been to take off in that car. Being a fourteen year old girl at the time, I was worried about being in trouble with the police for stealing a car. But looking back, it might have gotten me out of that whole mess altogether. Having definitely grabbed the attention of the officer, we would of had time to explain what had happened to us, and possibly been saved. But alas, no one would ever know. The chance had passed. So, off we went. Off to some unknown destination, without any idea of what was in store exactly.

We arrived several hours later at a facility called 'Brightway' in St. George, Utah. We pulled up to a bare looking building and entered the facility through a heavy door. We were told in advance we would be staying there until they sent us on to a more permanent facility.

Upon arrival I was led to the bathroom where I was instructed to take a shower. I was given lice shampoo to wash my hair with, and was watched as I bathed. I was inspected, naked, to ensure I didn't have any drugs or weapons on me. I then was put into a hospital gown. I was told I was there to be evaluated.

At that point, the place seemed legitimate, so I still had hope that maybe I wouldn't be sent away to a more permanent facility. I thought maybe the supposed professional psychologist that was supposed to evaluate me would put some sense into my father's head and let me go home. Years later I discovered that Brightway was owned by the WWASP Program, so an unbiased opinion of my behavior was not actually available. The place was not legitimate. This information was not made available to the parents. The whole place was a sham.

The Brightway facility was really more of a place for 'students' to adjust to the regime. There were a few options of where students would go after Brightway. Girls could go to Cross Creek in Utah or to Tranquility Bay in Jamaica. Boys could go to Paradise Cove in Samoa or Tranquility Bay. Those were the options at the time, but the program later expanded more on a global basis.

Brightway got kids familiar with the unreasonable structure, bare uncomfortable facilities, eating unappetizing food in silence, 'sharing' in group sessions, and getting used to the idea of having to follow pointless rules with firm consequences for violations of such.

I believe I only had one phone call while at Brightway, and it was in the office of their alleged mental health professional. The phone call was with my father. I wasn't allowed to talk to my mother because my father had full custody and he wouldn't allow it. Apparently, my mother, who I had been living with at the time prior to being 'escorted' to the Brightway facility, didn't know I was being sent away. This was all my father's doing.

The only time I left the Brightway facility was when I was taken into town to get my passport photo. They took me out in a hospital gown, and put a sweatshirt over it. I refused to smile for the picture. I still have the passport. I look extremely unhappy. Righteously so, under the circumstances. While the photo was taken simply as a head shot, the hospital gown pokes through sloppily at the top of the sweatshirt collar, crooked. It was crooked just like about everything else I experienced for the next two years.

I stayed at Brightway for a few weeks. Then it was time for me to go to their Tranquility Bay program in Jamaica. They drove me to the Las Vegas airport and put me on a flight with a layover in Miami, Florida. When I got off the plane in Miami, I was met by a security guard who escorted me around until I boarded my plane to Jamaica. Strangely, I don't think anyone in the airport knew what was going on.

7 – THE EXPERIENCE

'The program told the parents they made a responsible choice by 'saving us from sure death.' So, rather than open communication to try and heal the family, the blame was put onto the child.'

During my stay in Jamaica, I often looked forward to letters from home. I looked forward to them in the way a soldier off to war overseas looks forward to contact from the outside world. A letter from home gave me a distraction for a few minutes out of the day. With so little contact between 'students' and their parents, letter writing was the main form of communication. The students were not allowed to have access to the phone until reaching level 3 in the program. Even then, phone calls were only with parents, were arranged in advance and done in front of a case manager. Typically (if I recall correctly), phone calls were only done once every month or so, and limited to about fifteen minutes. It gave very little time to truly give parents a real understanding of what was really going on; or a chance for students to 'manipulate' as the program told parents, should anything negative be said about the program by the students.

So, writing letters was a main form of communication. Letters were turned into to case managers to review first, and then sent off to parents. While I think my case worker was probably a pretty honest one who had some genuine amount of caring for the kids in her assigned group, I think very likely other case managers reviewed letters, and withheld ones they didn't want parents reading that would reflect poorly on the program.

All letters in and all letters out went through the case manager. No one was allowed to send letters to friends, it was pretty much immediate family only, or whomever the parents designated as approved. Case workers were directed to send mail only to those that were on the list approved by each student's parents or legal guardians. The students did not have stamps, and were not allowed to possess them.

My father was so controlling he only allowed mail to go through him. He wanted all letters to and from my mother to go through his review first. He wanted to look them over prior to forwarding them in either direction. I still resent him for that. It is as though he was trying to punish my mother in some way; probably for leaving him. So, not only did he take me away from her, but he mediated our access to one another just to be spiteful.

My mother did not have much of a say in this, because my father had custody of me and she did not. Had my mother had her own lawyer when she divorced my father, she might had kept partial custody of me, and my father would not had been allowed to get away with sending me out of the country to an abusive reform school without her permission. My whole life might have been different.

If I were my mother I would had fought him legally stating that she was supposed to be permitted visitation, of which she was being denied. I wrote her letters telling her that she ought to talk to a lawyer. My father for some reason decided to allow those letters to be forwarded to her. Perhaps he knew she didn't have the money to hire an attorney to really fight him over it, so he humored it.

As difficult as the relationship with my mother is today, we were pretty close prior to me being sent away to Jamaica. Her letters to me were probably the only real thing that kept me going. On about a daily basis during my stay in Jamaica I thought about making a break for it away from staff and running up to the roof to jump, plummeting to my death. The only thing that kept me from doing that was the thought of making my mom sad if I were to die. So, I refrained from doing so.

I looked forward to getting letters from her, secretly hoping that she would be writing to me explaining that she found a way to bring me home. It never happened though. She spoke to a lawyer about me being sent away once or twice, but didn't have the money to continue the fight. There is one letter specifically that I will share later where it sounds as though she simply accepted defeat, and tried to console me to make the best of the situation. She at one point told me that maybe I could get some good out of being there. It was at that moment I understood clearly that she had given up fighting the circumstances.

The letters from my father and grandmother were for the most part insolent. Some were encouraging. However, I have an overall negative memory of them. Writing to me was their way of telling me what a horrible kid I was, and justified to them they had made the right decision in sending me there. There was almost no accountability on their part as to why I had turned out the way I had. I was simply on the receiving end of their venting. I read them anyway. I wasn't really allowed to write anything back to defend myself, because it would go through my case manager. Had I done so, I just would have been told I was trying to be manipulative or acting spoiled. It would have been brought up in group sessions by my case worker, and I would have to stand up and explain to everyone in group why I would do such a thing, and receive feedback. This was because I was to be held fully accountable for all of my actions, including the ones that led up to me being sent to the program. In my opinion, the program held the position that the child's behavior was completely the fault of the child, and the parents had little or no accountability. The program told the parents they made a responsible choice by 'saving us from sure death.' So, rather than open communication to try and heal the family, the blame was put onto the child. I truly believe that I was sent away to be fixed. The letters I received from my father and grandmother support that belief.

I sometimes received letters from my Aunts and Uncles, who were concerned about my stay there. I think it was probably equally alarming how vague my replies back to them were. The terminology I used was what now many of us survivors call 'programed.' I was literally brainwashed. I don't know if calling the program a cult is the specific word I would use, but it is the best I can come up with for lack of a better word.

In writing this book I asked for my letters that I sent home from Jamaica back from my Grandmother (Namma), who kept them all these years. She avoided the request for a while, saying she didn't have time to look for them. Eventually, she told me she gave them back to my father because he wanted to read them before they were given back to me. It was like a slap in the face. I felt like I was being censored by him all over again, just how it was arranged in the program. Knowing my father is a controlling, compulsive hoarder, I guessed he would take them from her, not read them, and lose them somewhere, causing them to not be found again. However, I did actually manage to get scanned copies of them about six months later.

I probably received over one-hundred letters from my family in my two year stay in the program. I decided to go through them as an adult. I've picked the ones that stood out the most to me. I found journaling to be a great tool for myself during my stay. I have heard others had their journals read by staff, and were often punished for what was written in them. However, I was fortunate enough to of never had to deal with that. I've included some of my journal entries and letters to and from home. I hope that in writing this book I am able to help others. Be it parents thinking about sending their child away, or other survivors of WWASP (or similar programs) to realize they aren't alone.

'April 17th, 1997

Dear Dad,

I don't know what you want me to say to you. You send me from place to place trying to fix me. I wish I could give you a bandage. I want you to know that I will always be who I am. I wish you could accept me for who I am rather than what you want me to be. I wish there was some way to get you to actually listen.

34

I understand that you see me as some rebellious kid that has no hopes and dreams, who just goes out and gets stoned all the time. I am more than you think I am. You never took the time to really understand me, or learn who I am. No one thinks I have any dreams. I do though. I want to join the U.S. Army when I am old enough.

I don't ever want to live with you again. I am not trying to disrespect anyone's feelings; I just don't want to live with you again. You just don't excommunicate your family and send them half way across the world. You have always tended to blame a lot of things on me, and that's not fair. You have been abusive for years, and that has a lot to do with what happened to our relationship. Just because you don't like the way your child turned out doesn't mean you blame them and give up on them. I can't live your dream of what you want me to be.

Cindy'

'May 16, 1997

Dear Cindy,

It was nice to get your letter. As you probably know it is hard to get much information about/from Jamaica. Every now and then I talk to your Case Manager, Patrice Dacey. She says you are OK but not working the program yet. (Also you are tanning). Please try to work, to go up the levels. I'm sure you are bright, and can do well.

We miss you, but we are sure this is the right thing for you. I tried everything else, but you never cooperated, even when it would've been fun! It was very frustrating when you and I first moved to Livermore. It seemed we would get along fine, making a house together. At first you helped with moving the furniture during our move to Livermore, and we went to the Shadow Cliffs Waterpark with the girl across the street, Lillie.

You seemed to be a noticed leader, and played well with all the kids on the block. But even then you were selfish, refused to even do your fair share. I remember unloading stuff (mine and yours) while you were playing. I guess no one ever taught you to be responsible, that being part of a family meant you have to pull your own weight, or more. I hope you will see that respect and trust are important, something you can earn, and keep earning.

You hurt me and my mother every time you refused to cooperate. I hope you see you even hurt yourself.

I remember when you and I were looking into the Cheerleader Class for you. I made a special trip the night before just to see where it was. I thought you would have fun, meet other girls, and make some friends. I was willing to drive you there before I went to work the first morning (and it was in the opposite direction of my drive to work on the other side of town). But in the morning you decided not to go. I never found out why. And you almost never cooperated on anything after that.

You would not go to violin lessons, even though I'd pay, and because you are talented you could've had fun. You and your friend from school refused to go to the Wednesday night youth group. You wouldn't join the Rainbow girls, even when it got you into the rodeo for free, and on and on.

I'm telling you all this because I want you to see it from my view. I tried, again and again, but you never cooperated. Not only that but it seemed like you messed up things. For example, the tutoring after school, the horse riding lessons in exchange for working on the ranch, the family counseling, your own therapist, one school after another.

When you were grounded you might go out the window. You seemed to have no respect for my mother and I, or for anything, food, the house.

You asked me from Brightway how long I've been planning this. Well, because of your attitude I've been building up to this, or someplace worse. It probably started when you refused to eat dinner with us. When you showed that you didn't want to be part of the family, it hurts us, too.

Despite all this I still love you, and want you back, but as part of the family. I don't understand why you are so angry. Or why you tell stories that are not true. Your mother for example. I never did any head-trips on you to make you mad at her. In fact, the opposite is true. She would call, and ask to speak to you. I would tell you, and ask you to talk, but you often would refuse. Or would begrudge her a few words, like 'Fine,' probably in answer to the question 'How are you?'

Your mother ran out on us, on me, and you. She said she didn't want any responsibility. It hurt, but I tried to do the best for you. Maybe you were mad at her, but couldn't yell at her, because she would just bring you back early, or hang up. Is that why you were so angry at me?

After sending you to the child's ward of the psychiatric hospital in Walnut Creek because you became suicidal, we decided to give you one last chance. You got to live with your Mother, you got a new school. But you argued, fought, went out the window, threw the phone, and failed almost everything in school.

Because I care about you, I knew you needed to learn you cannot succeed in life, unless you are responsible. If you will try, apply yourself, learn to appreciate all the love I have for you, and to give some back you will go on to have a better life. To do that you have to separate from bad influences, like drugs. Because your friend Tom is involved with drugs, you cannot write him. All letters to or from you must go through me, including the ones to and from your mother.

Changing habits and attitudes is not easy, and probably can't happen in a short time. You are not coming home until the program recommends you.

Love, Dad.'

My initial reaction to this letter was anger, injustice, and fear. My heart dropped into my stomach and I became very afraid of what was going to happen to me in Jamaica, and I worried about how long my stay might be there. In retrospect, my father had no business being in charge of a teenage girl. He clearly did not know his own child. He took no accountability for his part in the situation. He acted as though my depression was inconvenient to him and had no idea how to deal with it.

'May 2nd, 1997

Dear Namma,

When I come home, even if it is eighty degrees, I am going to be freezing! It is always around ninety-five degrees here, and it's humid. I got level 2 and only got one demerit all week! I can have these bag juice things now once a week. They are kind of like otter pops, but bigger. I have to get used to the food here. They often give us cabbage and boiled greens for breakfast. Well, I better go for now.

-Cindy'

'May 2nd, 1997

Dear Dad,

I don't have an issue with reasonable authority. The authority you were trying to assert was abusive. Today I learned in group that I am a tense and nervous person. I think it has a lot to do with you. You scared me. I am a mess. The abuse, hitting, yelling, threatening, stomping, chasing me around. I am tired of living a life of fear. You hurt me. You really did. I can try to forgive but I can never forget. Please write back.

Cindy'

'May 5th, 1997

Dear Dad,

I don't know what to say to you. Sometimes I hate that you sent me here. One of my friends here says that I am like a totally different person. I am still thinking about how I feel about that. Sometimes I am glad I am making changes in myself. Sometimes it freaks me out. I wonder what is happening, and if I am going to forget everything I care about. People use program lingo around here and it seems robotic. I don't want to be like that.

I changed rooms last night. I have a window next to my bed. I have a top bunk. I can hear the ocean and see the sun rise over the hill. It is nice.

I can see that I have some things that I need to work on. The biggest thing I want from the program is a relationship with you and my family. I want to know why you are not letting me have direct contact with my mother. I don't understand why you are doing it. I want to know if you are forwarding my mail that I send to my mother. Has my mother talked to you about custody?

Cindy'

'*June 8th, 1997*

Dear Dad,

You are in my prayers. I am upset with you. You didn't tell my mother you were sending me here and I didn't even get to say goodbye to her. You rushed me out of the house when you picked me up. It is very hard to forgive you for that.

I would like to come home. I am willing to accept discipline, but I do not agree with physical fighting. I am tired of the fighting and arguing and finger pointing. It makes me sick.

Cindy'

'*July 19th, 1997*

Hi, Cindy!

Just now finally got your letter from about a week after you graduated the Discovery Seminar. It is a beautiful letter, and the one I forwarded to your Mom is, too.

I'm very pleased that you learned so much, and seem to have done a lot of thinking. I got a lot out of the Discovery Seminar, and Focus Seminar as well. Who taught your seminar? Did some of the others get booted out of the seminar? I'm proud of you! I think there's a lot of good you can learn, but you have to want to. You can lead a horse to water but you can't make him think.

I learned that people do not see themselves as others see them. I learned that it is okay to share feelings and emotions, something I'm not very good at. Yes, I do want you to be happy, and a part of the family. I didn't like how you acted or some of the things that you were doing, but I always love you.

I don't understand why you say you never ate. I guess you never ate dinner with us as a family. Certainly you ate. You'd eat all of the ice cream and other junk in the house, and leave a mess, leave the milk and ice cream out. At that time you said to us, and to the councilors that you didn't want to be part of our family. That really hurt. That was one of the signs that something would really have to be done. Maybe you are changing your thoughts on that.

I'm sorry that you didn't get a chance to say goodbye to anyone, not even your mother. We really didn't have a chance to say goodbye to you, either.

I felt I had to keep the date a secret, because I was afraid you would have run, and probably gotten yourself into worse trouble. You know we tried everything and checked out a lot before we decided on the WWASP Program. It was really hard on me to see you off like that, and we waited anxiously for the phone call that said you'd gotten to Brightway okay. We repeated all that when you left for Jamaica. Put your feelings into another letter, and send it to your mother, through me.

I don't know if you will finish by the date marked on the return plane ticket, as you had inquired to me about. While parents do decide many things, it is up to you as to how fast you progress. I will respect the staff, and hope you are recommended home as soon as you can. The only way out is through. Maybe by the time this letter gets to you, you will already be on level three and we can talk on the phone. I am looking forward to talking to you again or maybe for the first time in a long time. Last I heard you had over 860 points, and things were going good.

How do you like the new facility? What is it like? We didn't know you moved facilities until we found out on the parents online support group. We talked to some other parents at the Focus Seminar about it too. They now have three phone lines and you can actually hear what is being said over the phone. I guess in Jamaica you have to buy a building to get a phone system. Also today we talked to the staff member Raymond, who is now helping with the facility in Utah. He remembered you!

Enclosed is a letter your Mom e-mailed to me at work, while she was visiting your Aunt Mackenzie.

Your Sensitive Loving Dad.'

I would like to post my feelings about these letters, as I have now had fifteen years to process them. As I have mentioned, my father is a compulsive hoarder. His idea of eating together as a family was to gather around the table, and eat along the outside edges of the table, because the rest of the table was piled with his clutter and garbage. I may not have known how to express it then, but no wonder I didn't want to eat dinner with him, or be a part of his family. There was something terribly wrong in the whole situation and he still didn't see it. He hoped that maybe I had changed my thinking about my home life since I was in such a desperate situation being in the program, where in his mind, I was getting fixed.

The lack of communication between the program and my father is pretty atrocious. I think it is incredibly irresponsible he was not notified personally, especially not ahead of time, that they were moving facilities. The different locations were on completely different parts of the island. If I were a parent, I would have wanted to know that information, and would have seen a giant red flag had that of occurred.

My father claims in the letter he did a lot of research about places prior to sending me away, yet he asks me what it is like there. I think it shows his lack of responsibility in all of this. I would never trust my child with strangers, and would never send them somewhere I had not seen and reviewed in person.

And lastly, I find it incredibly creepy the staff member Raymond remembered me. Years after my leaving the program it was found that he was accused of sexual abuse of a child. Allegedly, while a 'student' was in observation placement under his care, he forced the child to wear a garbage bag as a diaper, and when the child relieved himself, Raymond took him outside to spray him down with a garden hose and scrubbed his genitals with a toilet brush. He has continued to be in trouble with authorities on several other occasions involving abuse of children, being arrested and detained for third degree assault on a child and reckless endangerment (for putting a child at risk for bodily injury). Raymond has been accused of restraining a child for six hours at a time, causing physical abuse to the point of bleeding to children in his care, accused of forcing children to lie in their own blood, and has admitted on video tape to taking a part in pepper spraying a child multiple times a day for months. Even after accusations, the man still preyed on the troubled teen industry. He has since had some convictions. I do hope that when he is free he is not allowed to work with or be around children. He is a despicable human being in my opinion. And it is horrifying that he remembered me.

'July 6th, 1997

Dear Dad,

I've seen most of the girls arrive here except for about fifteen. There are about forty of us now. There are guys here, but we never get to do anything with them. We don't even get to see them. Ever. If we were to catch a glimpse of them we would get in big trouble and wind up with a Category 2 rule violation and be sent to worksheets.

We get to swim in the river next to the ocean on level two, but we don't get to go very often. I need 500 more merits to be on level 3. By the time you read this letter I should have the merits. However, it takes a lot more than merits to go up a level. It takes a lot of effort and perseverance.

I clean everyday here. I sweep, dust, mop, and arrange things. It is a bit difficult. Our daily schedule includes chores, meal times, school, fitness, group, singing and education video. We wear uniforms.

It's not so hard to get in touch with yourself once you let go of things inside. I feel you are holding on to all the pain I gave you. When you would look at your own daughter you saw what you did. That is not who I am now. That was never me; it was just a cover-up for how I was really feeling.

I have been working on sharing ideas and my feelings, as well as having faith in myself and my higher power, letting things go, forgiving, not beating myself up for mistakes, building relationships, and remembering who I really am inside.

I am learning how to not let things build up, because that is how I lost touch with myself. I became really angry. I am learning about myself and who I am, and am dealing with my past behaviors while learning what was behind them. I want to build trust with my family and mend the things that I can. I take responsibility for my actions and past behaviors.

I never felt reached out to by you. I always felt forced to do things. I want a relationship with you where we do things together and respect one another, and a relationship where we communicate.

I want to tell you the things that I have done in the past so that I can start to build your trust and respect back. I smoked pot, sometimes more than once a day. I smoked cigarettes. I have lied in the past. I have stolen money and cosmetics from people. I got in trouble for shoplifting once. I started drinking alcohol a month before I was sent here. I had people over in the house when I wasn't supposed to. I wanted to receive your love but didn't feel I deserved it. I was lost inside and didn't know where to turn, and didn't want to ask for help.

Cindy'

'July 20th, 1997

Dear Dad,

You wanted to know about my merits. I have about 1100. Being here in the program I have to be strong. This is the most difficult thing I have had to do in my life. The universe unfolds as it does, and everyone has a right to be in it. There are no accidents. I want you to know that you really scared me. Maybe that can answer some things for you.

Cindy'

'July 20th, 1997

Dear Namma,

The game we play is let's pretend. And pretend we're not pretending. We forget who we are and forget that we've forgotten. Who are we really? Our true center watches and runs the show. It chooses which way we will go. The 'I Am' is who we really are. It's the powerful, loving, perfect reflection of us. In our attempt to deal with situations we regress into a passive position. To avoid punishment we avoid our responsibility. We pretend that things just happen. We become comfortable with inflicting pain upon ourselves. We put ourselves down and become used to this posture. Weakness. Indecisiveness. In reality we are free. Your will is your power. Don't pretend you don't have it or you won't.

Cindy'

'July 27, 1997

Dear Namma,

I have learned that freedom doesn't mean not being locked up behind a fence, or having the choice on whether or not to leave. It's all about being free with yourself. I demand greatness from myself. It's up to me to earn the things in life I want, as I am the only person I can ultimately rely on. I am strong now, and proud of myself.

I miss being able to talk to you at night, or play cards with you. Remember when we read the newspaper together? It was fun when you would read my magazines. It showed you cared. I liked reading poems you wrote. Did you ever find Grandpas book of poems? I look forward to building a stronger relationship with you.

Love, Cindy'

'August 1st, 1997

Dear Dad,

I hope to be talking to you on the phone soon. I will be going up for my Level 3. I just need that to be approved by my group and case manager. If I get that I will be allowed to talk to you once a month. I want you to know it takes much more than merits to get through this program. The program isn't an insta-fix. Issues are still there. My feelings are still there, they didn't go away. Attitudes can change and reactions can change. I am not turning into a different person though. I am just demanding better of myself. When I come home, it isn't just about me acting different, but you acting different too.

Here in the program my group gets together to discuss what is working and what isn't working. We are there to try and support one another, and live up to what our group stands for. My group is named 'Alive.' We stand for Ambition, Love, Integrity, Vibrance and Energy.

I hope when I come home we can sit down and do something like that. Maybe we could get together on Saturdays and figure out what is working and what isn't, and divide the chores. Maybe once a month we could all go out as a family and do something fun together.

I've been getting to know people in the other girls group. We have a movie night on Saturdays. We all enjoy being able to talk to one another.

I volunteer in the kitchen when I can. It's fun. I help wash the dishes and the pots and pans. I help with sweeping and moping. There is a pot so big that I could probably fit into it if I crunched myself up into a ball.

When I come home I would like to get a job and build work experience for a resume.

Love, Cindy'

'August 3rd, 1997

Dear Dad,

I know I have been telling you all of the good things going on, but I haven't been telling you the things that are hard for me. I've been having a hard time hanging in there. It's hard for me to keep going on. I feel alone.

45

Sometimes I feel helpless. I feel like it doesn't matter what I do or say, that you will never see me as truthful. I am worried about how long I will be here because I don't know when I will be coming home. It's hard for me to want to change for myself, rather than just change so that I can go home.

I can't say that I have it all together because I don't. I see that my life before was a mess. I think about everything I left behind because the choices I made got me sent here. I feel so lost right now. I want to know that I am loved, cared for and important to you. Dad, you said you did everything you could to work with me. My point of view is that the biggest thing was overlooked. You didn't express that you love me. I want you to read something I wrote about our relationship:

When I was little my Dad and I got along well. He took me to the park and I helped him around the house. As time went by I began to see a different side to him. He started getting angry really easily, and that is when a lot of yelling and hitting started in the family. I guess it could be called a family secret, because no one in the family talked about it. I kept my mouth shut about it when I was little. The relationship with my Dad started falling apart after that. We never talked or played games after he came home from work like we used to. He started spending more time in his room. I'd sometimes ask him to play a game with me, but I had to initiate it. After a while, even that died out.

When my parents first separated, the only thing my father and I did together was watch an hour or so of television together. Our conversations became less and less. He would ask if my mother was over or not while he was out, and mentioned the houses he was looking at in Livermore that he was thinking about buying.

I felt like my family never really existed. We were only together, united, and healthy for a few years of my life. When my dad and I moved to Livermore it seemed like we might be in a position to have a better relationship. However, I became uncomfortable. I acted out as a defense mechanism. I wanted to be a force to be reckoned with because I didn't want to be in the same abusive situation as my mother. I was afraid of my father.

I don't know much about my father and what he is about, but I take accountability for not putting forth much effort to do so. We didn't have much of a relationship. We yelled and argued. I used to leave the house after verbal and physical fights. I'd call the police, but they never really did anything about it. I was hurt because I feared and was angry with my father, whom I should have wanted a relationship with. I'd like to build a relationship with him. One where I don't have to be afraid. I want to be able to express my frustration in a better way.

Cindy'

'August 24th, 1997

Dear Dad,

I passed the Focus Seminar. It was a really powerful experience for me. They did the seminar with the males in the facility. That was unusual, because we never get to spend time with them or see them. The facilitator of the seminar said I stood out to her, and that she was going to expect great things from me.

I wanted to talk to you about what our family was like. My Case Manager, Patrice Dacey said to me you told her there was no abuse in our family. The abuse in our family came up for me during the seminar. I want you to know that my Case Manager heard me talk about the abuse in our family during the seminar, and said in front of everybody that I was lying. I have lost trust with her and the other students there because of that. I encourage you to think about that.

I remember when I was smaller and my Mothers toe got slammed in the door accidently. I remember I was sent to my room and you slammed me up against the wall numerous times and punched me in the stomach.

I also remember seeing my mother being choked by you in front of my face. I remember the fights in the living room, the busted bathroom door, and the bruises my mother had. I remember going to the doctor and getting my arm x-rayed because I blocked you trying to strike me across my face. I remember my mother protecting you when the police asked if they wanted you arrested. She didn't do it because she didn't want you to lose your job. I remember my mother crying all the time. I remember how angry you were. It's all very real to me. I know it isn't anything for us to be proud of, but it is something that can't go away, even if not spoken about. I built up a lot of anger towards men because of these things.

47

I was suicidal even after leaving the children's mental health hospital in Walnut Creek. I cut myself with razors. I hated myself. I longed for a place where I felt like I belonged. I want you to know that I am ready for change in my life.

Cindy'

'*August 30th, 1997*

Dear Dad & Namma,

I was so happy to be able to talk to you on the phone. I know it was kind of odd for all of us. To me, just knowing my family was on the other side of the phone was enough for me. I didn't know what to say. It has been a really long time.

Today I helped clean up a puddle in the bathroom even though I didn't make it. And later on in the day I helped one of my group members. She was arguing with one of our roommates. They were arguing over something in the bathroom. I told the one who wasn't in the bathroom that I noticed she was getting frustrated. I asked her what happened. I told her fire doesn't put out fire, and that our roommate can give her an attitude, but that doesn't mean she has to give an attitude back. If we are nice to her and don't let her get to us, if she is still being mean, than that is her problem. My group member told me 'Thanks Cindy, I needed someone to tell me that.' It seemed to make the situation better. That felt good.

The food here, I don't personally like. The vegetarians get vegetables for breakfast a lot, and often times it is a lot of cabbage. We only get powdered milk to drink, or some sticky sort of juice. It takes a lot of getting used to. The bread I didn't like at first, but I like it now. It's hard to explain. It's like American bread, but it has less air and is really condensed. They do have really good fruit though.

Love, Cindy'

'*September 7th, 1997*

Dear Namma,

I miss my family. I miss American food, television, freedom, being able to make choices, being allowed to talk on the phone. I miss having free time and being able to spend time with friends. I miss wearing my own clothes and being able to wear make-up. I miss being able to go to bed when I want, and being able to sleep in on the weekends. I miss using a washing machine. I have to hand wash everything here in a bucket. I could walk around at home and look at the stars. I can't do that here. I can't cook here. I can't hug people without permission.

I beat myself up for the things I've done to be sent here. I hate being locked up. I feel like it will never end. I never imagined not being able to go home. I feel pushed aside. I feel like sending me out of the country is a way of rejecting me. I feel unwanted. I am frustrated but not allowed to express it here. I feel like giving up. I see myself being here for the rest of my life. I don't want to graduate the program on level 6. I really don't. I think my father thinks levels and points are everything, and like the staff recommending me home is like some sort of guarantee. It makes me feel sick. I am scared.

Cindy'

'September 14th, 1997

Dear Dad,

These are the things I didn't like about our relationship: We didn't communicate. You compared me to other people. Being hit and seeing you hit my mother. Your anger. The junk you continually collected and didn't do anything about. You being upset at me for playing with the kids in the neighborhood instead of helping you move your junk into the house when we moved even though I helped you many times before. When you isolated yourself in your room. When you found things for me to do that I wasn't interested in and got upset with me for not doing them.

Cindy'

'September 14th, 1997

Dear Cindy,

We went to the Parents Club, which was in Orinda yesterday. This is as close to Oakland as the Club has ever met. I told your Mom, and e-mailed the instructions. I did that for the last meeting, but this time your mother actually showed up. She brought her boyfriend Henry, and I think she learned a lot. I brought the sales tape the program sends to prospective parents, which shows Tranquility Bay as a tropical resort, with swimming, boating, volleyball, as well as studying, and it shows the rooms. We ran it there, so your mother and Henry could see what it looks like.

The program told me about the letter that was sent directly to you from your mother. I discussed it with her at the meeting. She has sent another letter to you, through me, and I have put it in the mail.

One thing that I'm learning from the program, and from writing letters to you, is that it is useful and good to put my thoughts into writing. The process helps me to clarify my own thinking, and is therapeutic. I received the letter you wrote about your feelings for me, and what went on when you were here.

I'm glad to hear some things from your side, but I do have some questions. It seems like you sometimes emphasize drugs, when drugs were a small issue. Why? For example, you say that when the Police caught you and Tom behind the liquor store, and I had to come and get you, that you were suspected of dealing drugs. Yet the Police told me the problem was you had alcohol, and were minors. I think you were thirteen at the time. If there had been any drugs, I'm sure they would have told me and probably taken you all to jail. Incidentally, they told me then they knew Tom from previous police encounters, but that it was the first time they'd caught you.

Maybe it sounds more prestigious to you to say you were involved with drugs? Who are you trying to convince, and what are you trying to convince us of?

Hope you're doing well. What do you have to do now to get to level 4? Are you making friends with the other kids? Does the fact that they keep adding new kids affect you?

You are in my thoughts!

Love, Dad.'

The video spoken of in this letter, like the brochure, didn't show anything that even involved their program. The brochure listed one far away photo of the building. The rest were all made up. Perhaps stock photos. Such as the picture of kids sitting in their own clothes on a comfortable cushy couch playing a guitar for 'music time.' There were no comfortable clothes; they wore uniforms. There were no instruments the school supplied. There were no cushy couches in painted rooms with art; there were hard plastic chairs in bare rooms with white walls. The plumbing didn't work in many instances, and human urine and feces piled up for days in the whole facility until it was fixed. I never once saw a boat or played volleyball. The school didn't have any sports equipment until my father sent some over. We played with the sports balls my father sent until they were flat, and then continued to play with them. Exercise was usually walking around a concrete yard filled with gravel, or student led activities like jumping jacks, squats, or abdominal crunches. At the second facility we did actually have a pool. However, because it was not maintained, it was lined with a thick layer of slime on the bottom, and we were not allowed to swim in it eventually. The truth was not exactly the resort that it was marketed as being.

While I am glad that my father was able to get some therapeutic value out of writing to me, he put himself first, and failed to actually consider how his words would affect me from across the miles. It is just one of the many ways he can be selfish; the very thing he repeatedly accused me of being.

'September 20th, 1997

Dear Cindy,

You told us the food wasn't very good there. Are you eating? I know that you didn't eat at home, and it was one of my worries. I knew about the cigarettes and thought you might have used a little marijuana but didn't realize the extent of it. I guess you're not eating should had been an indication. Are you a vegetarian now? If you are, we will have to devise menus that are well balanced when you return home. I understand that

51

beans are a good source of protein, but are incomplete and need some cheese to make them complete. Keep up the good work.

Lovingly, Namma'

It is disturbing to me that my grandmother, who was living with my father and handling the cooking at the time when I lived with him, didn't know that I was a vegetarian. I had gradually eliminated meat from my diet since the early age of five or six; when I learned that bacon is from a pig. I also find it disturbing that she didn't know that I was forced to eat fifty percent of my meals in Jamaica. The food was really horrible in the program

'September 29th, 1997

Dear Cindy,

It was good to receive your letter of August 20th, 1997. I am very proud that you have reached level three and I can see from your letters you have really made some good changes in yourself.

I'm glad that you have some goals set for when you return home. Goals can be reevaluated and changed later on as long as they are constructive in nature and help you to avoid unhealthy choices along the way.

I would very much like the opportunity to talk with you but it isn't likely for some time. Your father and I are at odds because he sent you away without my knowledge and I have resisted giving him any money for this and other reasons. He is running the show and I can't even send a letter to you directly without his censoring it and at the same time I don't get to read his letters to you.

Meanwhile, I am still trying to get my life back to normal here. I joined the City of Oakland's Job Asset Training Program, where I will get paid minimum wage for looking for work twenty hours a week. I think it is a good program for me because it requires me to document my job search and keep me on track as to how I use my time looking for work. I am presently having problems with filling out the forms to track my job search but feel that problem will pass shortly.

I talked with Granny and your Aunt. They seem to be doing well. It would be nice if you would drop them a letter along with your Aunt Mackenzie and Uncle Jack who are planning a trip to Jamaica in November. I'm sure they would like to see you while they are vacationing in Jamaica.

Guess I will close for now. I miss you.

All my love, Mom.'

Kids in the program were not allowed to have visitors, or leave the campus, except on very rare occasions with permission from the Program Director, and it had to be while in the custody of a staff member or immediate family member. It would have been nice to have seen my Aunt and Uncle, but they would not have been allowed into the facility. I recall there was an Aunt of an eighteen year old who had to get the authorities involved so that she could speak to her niece. She wanted to bring her niece home with her. She told her that she could go; that she didn't have to stay. The girl told her she was afraid her parents would disown her if she left, and she didn't know what she would do because she would be homeless. The program knew a lot of kids wanted to wait it out until they were eighteen years old so they could leave on their own freewill, so the program put together a plan with the parents called an 'exit plan.' The exit plan basically threatened to cut off the legally adult-child from the family and leave them completely on their own if they chose to leave the program without graduating when they were eighteen. This girl was really afraid of that happening. Her Aunt knew her niece was in an abusive situation, and tried to talk her into leaving, saying she would take care of her, and that she wouldn't be alone. Sadly, the girl decided to stay.

I think the program kept visitors out because they wanted to avoid those sorts of situations. They also didn't want people knowing what was going on behind their closed gates. They would be open and exposed if that happened, and they had a lot to hide.

One time they actually let a camera crew in from a major American news program. I'm not sure exactly how they managed to get the owner to agree. Years later I watched the video, which showed me from afar in my uniform on the exercise field. The children that were interviewed had been carefully selected by the program director. They were the 'good' ones, in his opinion, because they were compliant and would regard the program to the news crew in a positive manner. The airing of the special on Tranquility Bay wound up not going in the programs favor so much. It wasn't until many years later any other sort of news program was allowed into the facility again.

'September 30th, 1997

Dear Cindy,

I know your life is full of ups and downs. Sometimes it looks like a lot of downs. In life there are certain things a person has to decide to do, and not do, if they want to succeed. In life, there are consequences. I'm afraid you were able to squeak though junior high school, even though you didn't do all of the work. This is just a sign of the failure of the school system, not an example of good training. In real life, if you don't do the work, you don't keep a job. If you don't finish school it will be very hard to even get a job. At the program they maintain structure, and from your letters I see that you are seeing some of the things they are showing you.

I know the program can be hard. It is not easy to examine yourself, to face the real you. No one is perfect. First you have to discover what is good, and what is bad about yourself, and then decide what you want to make of yourself.

Your wrote me about the time you slammed a door or your mothers foot (by accident). *You and your mother used to yell a lot, and I didn't know how to stop it, but it had never before gone so far. My memory of the incident is that you started out very angry, defiant, and that you ran into your room, and then deliberately slammed the door on your mother's foot. It was so hard that I had to take her to the hospital. Her foot might have been broken. She was crying in pain. You deliberately hurting one of us, your Mother, my then Wife, was terribly upsetting to me. It was like you were a wild animal, not civilized. At first I couldn't understand that you would do such a thing. Did you think hurting people is like the TV cartoons you watched often, where the coyote is okay right after being pushed off a cliff? Then I became enraged, and yes, I probably lost it. I had to take your mother to the hospital, and didn't take the time to sit down and have a courteous discussion. I remember grabbing you and demanding to know why you did it. You yelled something back, and I remember pushing you up against the wall, and telling you to never do anything like that again. Cindy, this happened once, and is not the way a family should be. It is not how I like to think of myself and it is not how I like to think about you. It is not the way I hope us to be in the future.*

Change is inevitable (except from a vending machine).

Don't get any ideas about getting out early. We miss you a lot, but we want you to finish and be like the girls we meet at the parents club: happy and confident, respectable and honorable.

I'm working on doing some changes too. I am going to counseling. I'm meeting with a group of parents, and I'm reading several books. As I learn more, I'm changing the way I think. It is hard to imagine how I can interact with you, because I keep thinking of you as you were before you left. It may be a lot different when you come back as the 'new' Cindy. I will be different, too. But I know it may not be easy, for any of us.

I do love you very much, and I care about you. I believe you have the power to succeed at whatever you want to do.

Love, Dad.'

The incident mentioned about my mother's foot getting slammed into the door was an accident. I never intended to intentionally hurt her. My father was so enraged he threw me up against the wall and punched me in the stomach repeatedly. He then would leave, just to later come back to physically abuse me further. It was not an isolated incident. The fact that he would do that to his own child is not any less animalistic than he accused me of being. He was an adult; I was a child at the time. It was his job to be the parent. He should have been responsible enough to be patient, and civil. But he beat his own child instead. It wasn't uncommon for him to lose his patience and resort to physical violence. I recall one time we were in his truck, waiting on my mother to get out the door so we could go. I must have done or said something that ticked him off, and he shook me then and there on the bench seat of his truck with his hands grasped around my neck. I also recall him trying to strangle my mother with a telephone cord once. And he was often physically violent with her after I went to sleep. I remember hearing her being thrown up against the wall and seeing bruises on her chest. I was so relieved when she finally left him. He hit me a lot as a child, and more so as an adolescent; likely because I no longer had my mother around to intervene. For him to only see his violence as an isolated incident is bullshit.

He then goes on in the letter to talk about me being a new person. Confirming my theory that he sent me to the program to be fixed. While perhaps he did some reflecting on his own time in regards to his own life, he is still basically the same person, minus the physical abuse.

October 12th, 1997

Dear Callie,

Please help me. My father has been procrastinating sending me a package and I am very hairy. Could you please send me an electric razor? I haven't shaved in nearly six months.

I see ocean crabs here a lot. They are really cute and sometimes fun to pester. One time I had to catch one in a cup and send him outside because simply he had to go.

They are getting cameras all over the facility. It feels weird and I don't like it. Wherever I go there is a new one by the time I turn around. It's crazy.

Cindy'

'October 12th, 1997

Dear Dad,

I've learned to be really quiet here and I don't speak up very often. A lot of the time I don't feel very important here. I spent time around Tom a lot at home because I knew he liked my company. He and his mother and their friends considered me family. I felt important.

Cindy'

'October 20th, 1997

Dear Namma,

Today is a Jamaican Holiday, so we have a Sunday schedule. One of the staff let one of the girls cut my hair last night. My hair has been really terrible since being at Brightway, because the lice shampoo I had to use turned it orange. My hair is really short now. All the girls like it.

My favorite staff member quit about 1 month ago. I am not happy about that. I dislike most of the staff. It seems like most of the staff are afraid to get to know us, and are pretty rash with us. A few of them are really nice though.

We have 49 pages of rules here, plus all the ones the staff make up. Anyhow, I better get going.

Cindy'

'October 26th, 1997

Dear Namma,

Thank you for the package you and Callie put together for me. I can't keep candy long. We aren't allowed to keep it overnight, so I shared it with the other girls in my group. We started a Tranquility Bay Paper recently. They put in a mention about me as 'Most Improved Hair' because of my haircut. They were going to put me in as 'Best Hair' but I don't know what happened.

Love, Cindy'

'October 26th, 1997

Dear Dad,

I was accused of cheating and got a Category 3 rule violation. The test had two answers that were right, and I went to talk to the staff about it. I was trying to explain why I thought both answers were right. The principal saw me talking to the staff and said I cheated because I was talking while I was taking a test. I am now back on Level 1 with zero merits. I thought I would get to talk to you before my birthday, but this changes things.

Sure, this is a setback. But I have gotten over it. I know the staff here thinks a lot of me and I know they were all real disappointed to find out I was dropped. I also know a lot of girls look up to me and I have built trust. I will handle the situation the best I can. I know you must be disappointed. I am a little discouraged, but optimistic.

Cindy'

Unfortunately, I only have letters that I sent in the year 1997. The rest, I believe have been misplaced somewhere in my father's house. I feel even though part of the history is incomplete, it is fantastic to be able to at least put some of these pieces together.

'November 15th, 1997

Dear Daughter,

I have been thinking about the holidays and how empty it is going to be without you. I also miss hearing your voice and being able to give you hugs.

I have been looking into getting more legal advice but my resources are limited since I have not been working full-time. I talked with a lawyer recently. Since your father has both legal and physical custody, my recourse may be limited. The lawyer said that she would have to look at the custody agreement.

Love, Mom'

'December 14th, 1997

Dear Cindy,

This is a note to let you know how much I love you and miss you. In a few days it will be Christmas, but I am having difficulty dealing with the festivities of the season. I have been trying to dwell with the spiritual meaning of Christmas, which is the birth of Jesus Christ.

I know you have been very lonely but it would be nice to know more about your feelings and experiences in the program. You have not shared anything with me.

I think that Henry will be coming here for the holidays.

All my love, Mom'

'December 14th, 1997

Dear Journal,

I wrote to my Dad today. I was really mad and upset. I want to hurt him as much as he has hurt me, and other people, like my Mom. Two days ago was my 8th month anniversary being here. It is so crazy this world. I wish I would still be talked about in conversations by my friends at home, but deep down I think people have stopped wondering what has happened to me, and have probably forgotten me. I miss my Mom. I want to go home. I hope she goes to court and gets custody of me, and brings me home.'

'December 21st, 1997

Hi, Cindy

I've been meaning to ask you what you eat. Is the food good? At one time you didn't want to eat chicken.

I know x-mas can be a sad time of year for Catholics. Your mother was always depressed around this time, and she walked out and left us at this time of year. Thank you for telling me her father died then. Somehow I never knew that.

It is very hard on Jewish people, too, especially when you live in an overwhelmingly Christian society. We refer to it as the December Dilemma. Everywhere you look there are neon Santa's, and cardboard nativity scenes, they play Catholic songs until you are sick of them. Each year they start this nonsense earlier until now it's almost before Thanksgiving. Even schools and governments, who are supposed to respect other religions, and keep church and state separate, seem to conveniently 'forget' around x-mas, and plaster the place with very Christian icons. These people can be overwhelming with their Merry Christmas's without regard for those who don't share their beliefs.

Maybe you can understand that we never had a tree when I was growing up. The whole idea of cutting down forests, dragging a tree inside where it dries up and becomes a fire hazard, and then throwing it out to litter the world is ridiculous.

So, when your mother and I married, we agreed that we would alternate holidays, and only have a tree every other year, and NO crossed or other Christian icons in the house but your mother wouldn't keep up her end of the deal. The first year I found out that I got very allergic with a real tree, so we decided to get an artificial tree. I bought one at a garage sale and she insisted on putting it up the second year. I said okay, but only if it would have the Jewish star. Every year it got worse and worse. To me it seemed that the Christians were invading my own home. That is why when your mother took down the Jewish star, and put up the angel ornament, I really felt I had to draw the line, the thing had gone too far.

I know you never learned much about the Jewish religion, and I'm sorry about that. We have a strong and rich heritage, you should be proud to carry on. I foolishly thought that would wait until you were old enough to understand, and make your own choice. It was my intention to take you to many different churches and temples, so you could see for yourself. I think all religions believe in the same God, no matter what they call him.

But your mother took you to church whether you wanted to or not. I had hoped that you would understand there are so many Jews who have made a difference in this world, and why we are still strong and proud, even though some people discriminate against us.

One of my concerns with you being there is that they will do the same about Christmas that folks do here, and expect everyone to participate in their holiday. Because they make an exception to many of their rules and schedule at Christmas is one reason I'm concerned. Well, there is not really much I can do about it, so I hope you make the best of it.

In one letter you ask again, 'How long will I be here.' The answer is the same: It depends on you, and on how fast you work the program and get recommended home.

I am hoping to talk to your case manager tomorrow, and maybe even to you as well.

My Love, Dad'

How my father was married to my mother for fifteen plus years, and didn't know that her father had died around that time of year is astounding. It goes to show how non-observant he was of other people.

For someone who was so upset about religion, he should had known what he was getting into when he married my mother, who was not Jewish, like he is. My father greatly resented my mother teaching me about her religion, yet he never took the time to teach me about his. The few times we went to temple I believe it was my mother's idea. I had asked about going to take classes at the temple to learn about the Jewish religion, but my father never made any attempt to arrange for it.

He took down our Christmas tree several times while my mother and I were out of the house. One time he put a sheet over the tree. It was a blatant disrespect and lack of tolerance that he displayed for my mother's beliefs. Yet, he always expected to be honored and respected, despite the way he treated other people.

When I think about it now, I am able to laugh about how ridiculous it all is. I suppose I'd just cry otherwise.

'December 31st, 1997

Dear Cindy,

I'm glad I got to finally talk with you the other day. You sounded good but your conversation seemed limited because you need to be careful about what you said about the Tranquility Bay program. I'm proud of you. You seem to be doing fine in the program. Your grades are good but I have heard that you need to take the courses that will keep you on track to being in the appropriate grade level.

Henry arrived in town a few days ago. I am doing well. I started working for a trucking company just before Christmas. It is a 60 day probation period of employment to see if things work out well. Guess I will close for now.

Love and Prayers, Mom'

If it was apparent to my mother in our fifteen minute phone conversation (the first of our phone calls in nearly nine months) that I was filtering my conversation, I simply do not understand how my father and grandmother did not detect this, and see it as a red flag. I suppose they wanted to believe they were doing the right thing. I think it just goes to show how little attention they actually paid to understanding me. Perhaps the next letter will better explain how even blunt conversation was blatantly disregarded.

'January 5th, 1998

Dearest Cindy,

I am quite disturbed about a recent letter you wrote. You write that you are in prison and that we do not acknowledge the progress you made. I know that where you are is strictly structured, and it is not great being there. But I also read the letters you wrote that told of what you were doing at home before you left. Your Dad certainly did not send you away out of hate. It was out of love. He felt that he was saving you from real prison or from death itself. He felt he was saving your life. He made all kinds of inquiries and chose the place he felt was best. He agonized and worried. He loves you and wanted to save you. Tell me, if he had asked you to join this program voluntarily, would you have gone?

It is true; you are not court ordered to be there. But, we have learned from going to the parent support meetings that teens who come back before they are recommended do not do well at home when they have to face the real world and all its temptations. We have talked with teens that have come back. What would the point of your being there and going through all you have gone through, if when you return, it didn't work? We do not expect you to be perfect or fixed, as you put it. We hope that you will have the skills to survive intact in this very difficult world to grow up in. You Dad loves you very much and wants for you only the best.

I know there will be many times when you will feel unhappy, but please try to see the other side. Work on yourself so that when you come home, life will be better for the whole family. We too are working on ourselves to learn more about ourselves and how to improve the family relationship.

All my love, Namma'

'January 15th, 1998

Dear Journal,

Sometimes I wish my father were dead so that I could go home to live with my mother. I hate him. I feel empty. It's pointless to keep me here because I am not going to change for myself. The only reason that I make any changes is so that I can have my physical freedom. I am trapped here. I feel like I am locked up like a caged animal. I am watched and censored and poked and prodded like some sort of experimental lab rat. I feel numb. I feel numb to everything. I want this nightmare to end. I have had enough of this. This is no way to live. My life is being wasted here. I think about killing myself so that I don't have to live this way anymore, but I am too afraid to die.'

'*February 8th, 1998*

Dear Journal,

There was only a level three activity for 15 minutes today. We waited so long for one, and 15 minutes is all we got. My father pays for this place out of my college fund. I hate my father. I don't want to give him another chance. I think it is sick the way he acts as if he is giving me another chance.'

'*March 8th, 1998,*

Dear Journal,

Nobody deserves to be in a place like this, especially for so long. Lord help give me guidance. Help me to have strength and courage.'

'*March 10th, 1998,*

Dear Journal,

We had water this morning, but only outside on the ground floor. It hasn't been working for days, not even outside. I was so excited that we had water that I forgot my toothbrush when I went outside to brush my teeth. I got some toothpaste from a girl in my group, and I think I did a pretty good job brushing my teeth with my finger.'

'*March 11th, 1998*

Dear Journal,

I woke up and the facility is without much water and has no electricity. The toilets are piled high with sewage because we haven't been able to flush them. There is never hot water.'

'March 13th, 1998

Dear Journal,

I talked to Namma today. She is pretty upset with me and said she would keep me here until I am 18 years old if necessary. I think I would probably jump off the roof and kill myself before I would let that happen. I'm serious. She won't even consider sending me to a better center, like one in California. She says I am sitting on my ass, and that I must like it in Jamaica.'

'March 14th, 1998

Dear Journal,

Today was the most boring day. I sat for nine straight hours because someone else ran away from the facility. I wonder who it was that ran away, and what they are doing right now. My head hurts and my brain feels fried from being so bored.'

'March 19th, 1998

Dear Journal,

I shaved last night. My legs look very skinny and my armpits are no longer hairy. I am supposed to talk to my Dad next week, but I almost don't even want to bother. I know I am supposed to need him, but I don't feel like writing him, or talking to him. I don't want to be around him at home. He gets everything he wants, especially over the last year with leaving me here. I am tired of giving him the satisfaction.'

'April 15th, 1998

Dear Journal,

The program director is trying to make some improvements with the food. It's about damn time, because the food has been so bad a girl fucking starved herself.'

'*May 20th, 1998*

Dear Cindy,

    I didn't find out that you were sent away to Jamaica until I called and talked with Namma that Sunday evening of April 13th, 1997. I told her I was coming to pick you up from your weekend visit with your father and she informed me that you were escorted out and sent to Brightway in Utah for holding. I can imagine how frightening this experience must have been for you. I first thought that you were going to Utah for a few months but when I received your letter telling me that you were being aired out of the country, it was startling. I went to bed and slept on the strange turn of events. I woke up the next morning and cried out my feelings for a while. I couldn't believe that your father would have you sent off out of the country without consulting me or talking with me about his plans. I think that you will benefit from this experience in that it will give you some lifelong tools to use in relationships with other people. Guess I will close for now.

    I miss you a bunch and love you. Mom.'

'*June 30th, 1998*

Dear Journal,

    I got dropped from level 4 last night. Apparently, it was because I have no confidence in myself. It wasn't because I had broken any rules. It's so unjust.'

'*July 21st, 1998*

Dear Cindy,

    Cindy, you have so many good qualities to feel good about yourself. Let me mention just a few. You have determination and confidence to try new things. You are artistic and can paint and draw far better than most. You are musical and can sing. These qualities I particularly admire because I don't have them. I can't draw beyond a stick figure and can't sing at all, although I enjoy music. I consider these lacks as handicaps. You are pretty, but most importantly, you have a loving heart and can empathize or understand others feelings. So feel good about yourself from the inside.

When we feel good about ourselves, we attract other people. They feel it. You can be a leader and help others instead of being the needy one. I think you are already feeling that. How lucky you are to gain these insights now so that you can use them the rest of your life. Teen years are difficult and our society now makes them even more difficult. But if you set goals for yourself and have confidence in yourself, you'll make it.

Cindy, you are loved. All my love, Namma.'

8 - THE CHANGE FOR ONESELF

'I see that I have a hard time being in touch with emotions other than being angry or upset.'

It took me a long time to get to upper levels. Over a year. When I finally got it, I had it only a couple months at most before it was taken away from me by their program director. I hadn't broken any of the rules. I was told by the administration that I just hadn't been 'working the program' in the way I should had, and was given group feedback. It was very vague, and I still do not understand why I was dropped. I was crushed.

I became very angry after that, and defiant. Anger and defiance were not tolerated in the program, and I was sent into observation placement for several weeks due to acting out. In observation placement I was put in a room with a tile floor while being overlooked by a staff member. I was instructed to lie on the floor on my stomach on top of my bathing towel. That is what I did all day, for hours upon hours. I was only allowed as instructed to do so, jumping jacks in place and stretching every few hours. If I were to defy lying down; which I tested; I would be restrained to the ground by two or three Jamaican women. They would grind my cheek and hips into the ground, and twist my arm behind my back so hard it inflicted pain. Some children were pepper-sprayed into submission. I was at least lucky enough to have avoided being sprayed. If I needed to go to the bathroom, I had to leave the door open, and be watched. When it was time to eat, I ate in the same room I laid in all day and was given food to eat out of a bowl with no utensils. People were shocked when I went into observation placement. I had been such an honest, good kid while I was there. I followed the rules and did as I was told. It was unlike me to act out.

I think I became a lot of fun after I was in observation placement. I had nothing left to lose in terms of levels or merits after I got out, so I said what I thought (what most students were probably thinking but restrained themselves from saying). My big mouth got me into a lot of trouble. I was in and out of worksheets a lot for a couple months.

'August 4th, 1998

Dear Journal,

I went to worksheets today. I got in fairly big trouble. I called a staff member a stupid bitch. I'd actually tell lots of people off around here and swear if I didn't get into trouble. There are some things I want to improve within myself. I want to be better able to communicate. I want to have confidence in myself. I want to be happy. I want to be doing well in school. I see that I have a hard time being in touch with emotions other than being angry or upset.'

My father came to visit just as I was getting back on track. Apparently, he had planned to come visit me after I had made the upper levels. He was going to take me off grounds. However, since I had dropped levels, I wasn't technically supposed to see him under the programs rules. He had already bought the ticket though, and decided to pay me a visit anyway. We spent time together on the facility grounds for several days.

He asked a former student whose parents he was in contact with what to expect when he came to see me at the facility. He was told to expect it to be rustic, dirty, and very structured. He was also told the food was terrible. I believe his experience met those expectations.

I did much better after he visited. I really made the effort to change, and became a part of things. I moved up levels one through three quickly, and my father made plans to have me transferred to a new associate program in Montana. The transfer was meant to be a transitional phase for me, so that I could adjust back into a more normal life and soon go back home.

'August 30th, 1998

Hi, Cindy!

I've been thinking about you since I saw you. I need to tell you straight out, so that you can't miss the point: You are not the reason your mother and I got divorced. The divorce is not your fault. What we did, we did as two adults who had a problem. I guess I never saw things from your mother's point of view. The main problems were her failure to understand or respect my religion, and her failure to stand by me.

I guess she felt that because I didn't go to temple and didn't worship in church, like she did, that my religion was not important. She was wrong. She knew very little about my religion. Your mother never understood the Jewish religion, and the Jewish culture. She insisted on forcing her Catholic religion on you, without asking me, because she knew from our agreements before we were married that I did not want to raise any more Catholics.

One day when you were a baby, while I was at work and she was at home, she and one of her girlfriends took you off to a Catholic Church, and had you secretly baptized. She didn't even tell me what she had done, but she took a picture and left it on the kitchen table. When I found out about it, I dried you off, and asked God to forgive her.

Later, she started sending you to Catholicism classes, also secretly.

I always felt that your mother and I should be united with regard to you, so I didn't discuss these things with you. Besides, you were just an infant, at first. When she wanted to take you to church, I did not interfere. I thought that when you were old enough, you should be able to make your own decision. But I was wrong. They got to you first, and force fed their religion into you, so that is all you know. Now you can't make an intelligent decision, because I doubt you know much about the Jewish religion.

When your mother took you to be secretly baptized, I didn't realize it at the time, but it showed that she could not be trusted on a very important issue, and that she didn't respect me, her husband. Later she did more and more disrespectful things that eventually destroyed the marriage.

My housekeeping was a problem, but that alone is not what destroyed the marriage. We had been together for many years.

I received your letter basically saying that you had been there for so long that you aren't going to try anymore. Cindy, I know you can work the program. You did it before, but I don't think that you did it for yourself. Please do everything you can, so you can move up the levels, and can come back a success.

Love, Dad'

The letter I feel shows good examples in regards to how my father thinks. In my opinion, he does not take accountability for his own actions, lack of actions, or contributions to his life or the lives of other people. He acts as though he had no part in his marriage falling apart, that his compulsive hoarding was just a simple housekeeping issue, and that in order to make things happen in his life that he wanted, such as teaching me about his religion, that he didn't have to actually make the effort to teach me about it.

As an adult, looking back on this, I feel as though my father used me as a pawn to get back at my mother. She had me baptized without consulting him first about it, and he in turn sent me out of the country without telling her about it. He calls her act disrespect to him. I suppose in his mind his act of sending me away was a disrespect towards my Mother. It is a shame to have a child in the center of tit for tat. He sent me away to Jamaica and limited our communication partially to get back at my Mother for divorcing him. He repeated a similar action when he refused to let me and his exfiancé; Callie; communicate with each other after they broke up.

'October 1ˢᵗ, 1998

My Dearest Cindy,

I think of you across the miles. Even though we are apart I think of you fondly and feel close to you. As you may know, your father and I are not together anymore. People need to find the kind of person they can relate to. I came to the conclusion that he and I are not suited for each other. I want to be adored and feel special, and I trust that someday you will choose the kind of person you deserve.

Because of the way the program is structured, it's difficult to write to you directly. Your father will not give me any letters from you. I hope that someday when you can choose to do as you wish that I will hear from you. I pray for your every success, and I know that you have the potential to achieve whatever you choose in life. Opt for the best with a positive 'can do' attitude.

With lots of love, your friend, Callie.'

'October 15ᵗʰ, 1998

Dear Journal,

A few days ago I went up for level 4. I got my groups support and my case managers, as well as my staffs support and the support of the principal. The junior staff all denied me support except for the ones in my group. What they said was complete crap. And someone had the nerve to say to me that I am lying to myself about being ready for level 4. I have worked my ass off trying to get it. I've even put together 'spirit days' for the lower level girls so that I can stand out as a leader. It's such bullshit! They just don't like me.'

'October 28ᵗʰ, 1998

Dear Journal,

I got level 4 back the day I left for the airport to leave Jamaica for the Parent Child Seminar #1 in Utah. Everyone except the corrupt student counsel supported me on my vote-up paper. Because they didn't approve, I shouldn't have been promoted to level 4. However, the program director made an exception for me, and approved my level advance an hour before I left for the airport. Leaving the Program in Jamaica was probably the best day of my life.

Since being back in America, I have eaten so much good food! When I got off the plane the group of us that arrived from the Program in Jamaica was greeted with applause. I saw my Dad, Mom and Namma there. When we got to the hotel I stayed in a room with my Mom. The first thing I did was take a bath. There were only cold showers in Jamaica, so it was so nice to take a warm bath. Today, I got my hair cut. I got to go shopping with my Mom and got a pair of really cool shoes. I also got to see Henry today. I am transferring to the facility in Montana. I just feel on top of the world!

9 - MONTANA

'These seemingly normal activities would never have happened for me in Jamaica.'

When I went to Montana, I initially got sick. The weather change from extreme hot to extreme cold really got to me physically, and I was ill for weeks. During those first few weeks, I got to know more about the people and the facility in Montana. Montana was a big change from Jamaica. I learned the staff seemed to actually care about the kids there, and were much more fair and easy to deal with than the staff in Jamaica.

I lived in a house with several other girls about 10 miles from campus. I rode in a van every day to and from campus to go to school and to participate in activities. While I still think my education lacked, as everything was done independently, if I needed help I could ask a teacher and was able to get some actual help.

Montana was still structured. However, it was a walk in the park in comparison to Jamaica. In Montana I got to do things like ride on a quad, babysit the directors kids, cook, go off grounds for fun activities, got to work out at a real gym, participated in things in the community, went to a high school dance with actual high school kids, went to basketball games and played laser tag. I went to bonfires. I got to be friends with boys. These seemingly normal activities would never have happened for me in Jamaica. It really meant a lot to me.

Montana was like summer camp in comparison to Jamaica. I really liked it there. I felt cared about. I was happy. I felt like an actual human being rather than a sad, neglected, caged animal. I wish that I had been sent there long before I was.

It wasn't so much that I wasn't willing to examine my own life while I was in Jamaica that held me back. It was the fact that there were no real outlets for change available for me there. In my opinion, it was a lose-lose situation there for the kids. I think just about everyone knew it. The kids who got ahead there were the ones who were in cliques, who were able to fake it enough until they got out. They were able to get away with not following the rules because of the permissions they were allowed in the upper levels. They didn't have as much supervision, so many of the things they did stayed under wraps in their cliques.

I wound up being an honest kid. Mostly out of fear for the consequences of lying, but nonetheless an honest kid. The upper level kids knew this about me. Therefore, they wouldn't vote me up because they didn't want me ratting them out, which is why it took so long for me to get to upper levels.

Motivation to genuinely change oneself in such an awful situation I think is unrealistic. While there was a rigid amount of structure in Jamaica, the whole situation was completely chaotic. Everything was unfair. The staff was incompetent as well as any medical personnel made available to the kids. Once, a friend of mine was forced to take medication she was allergic to. She was then stood up in group and given feedback saying she took it on purpose in an effort to be pulled out of the program early. Had she refused to take the medication however, she would have had serious consequences for refusing to follow staff orders. It was not a situation she could have won. In addition to problems like this there was not a licensed therapist or psychologist on staff in Jamaica. The parents were not actively involved.

Montana was different. I felt like I was treated as though I actually mattered. I felt like I was more than just a number in the headcount. The kids there also seemed to be way less intense than in the Jamaica program. The approach was less intense in Montana.

I felt like the staff actually cared about me doing well. I was even welcomed into their homes, which would have never happened in Jamaica. On the weekends, I got an actual day off where I typically stayed in the house with my group of upper level girls. We took turns cooking. We did one another's makeup. We had a bathroom with an actual bath in it and hot water. I was allowed to look out the window. More than just looking out the window, I got to wander off and actually explore the property around the cabin.

I made friends with a girl named Carrie. We had very similar personalities, and were often mistaken for one another, or asked if we were related. We still keep in touch to this day, and I consider her a dear friend. Even though we are half way across the world from one another as of this moment, she and I still tend to find our interests and path's to be very similar.

'January 2nd, 1999

Dear Cindy,

I was happy to be able to talk to you over the phone Christmas Day. I have further thoughts about your desire to live with me and not your father. Things are not definite with me. You may need to stay with your father until I get settled somewhere, as I am planning to sell the house, and I know that you don't want to go to public school in Oakland. The schools in Livermore where you father is living have a higher learning standard than Oakland schools, which is another reason for you to live there with him.

As far as your room at your father's house, it has some boxes of your belongings, and there are also boxes your father put in there that have computers and such, which I think he can easily move somewhere else.

I received a call from the Census Bureau just before Christmas. There is a chance I will be working for them on a temporary basis. The Bureau is looking for people to work as enumerators to perform household census for the year 2000.

Guess I will close for now. All my love, Mom.'

The example my mother gives in this letter stating that my father was hoarding computers in my room illustrates how my father still did not deal with his compulsive hoarding problem; a cause of major upset in the family dynamics for as long as I can remember. He sent me away to reform school to try and 'fix me' so that I wouldn't be angry about it anymore. And in return, he would do nothing about his actual problem that affected me so much. He figured he put a roof over my head, and that it didn't matter what or how much was under that roof.

I think this letter also shows how up in the air my mother's life was during the time I was away in the program. My mother did receive the house I grew up in as a child through their divorce settlement; however, it had not been paid off. She was not left with a lot of other resources, and she had a hard time finding work. I learned years later that my fathers combined assets were in the multi-millions. My mother had no idea.

In all of this, my father expected my mother to pay him back for half of the costs of him sending me away to the program. This was despite the fact that she was poor, had no say in the matter, and was not allowed to contact me except through him. He still until recent times brought up how (he feels) my mother owes him money for sending me to the WWASP Program. If I've needed something from him he tells me I should talk to my mother about it 'because she owes him money for sending me to the Program.' He did this all throughout my college years when I depended on him and my mother financially and at times when I needed help with health care expenses.

'January 5ᵗʰ, 1999

Dear Journal,

Happy New Year! I got to go to a high school dance at the town high school with the other upper level kids for New Years. Two boys asked me to dance. So much fun! Also, I am living in a house off campus. I really like the program in Montana a lot better.'

'January 19*th*, 1999

Dear Journal

I will be going up for level 5 this coming Monday. I am going on home pass soon! They won't tell me when exactly, but I am super excited. We will be working on a home contract.'

'February 21*st*, 1999

Dear Journal,

Home pass was hard. The house is gross. My Dad and I got in some arguments and I acted rudely at times. My Mom and I made some improvements and are working together. I cooked her dinner two nights. I got to stay with her for a few days. I found a school I want to go to. I discovered my old pipes that I smoked weed in. I threw them in the trash. It was a hard thing to do but I felt better afterword. I didn't get level 5 at vote up last month, but I am going to try again tomorrow. I left for home pass with another student here. We were picked up by the parents of a lower level student, and stayed with them overnight. I think it was because of some sort of flight layover.

Today I helped wash the facility van with another upper level. It was fun. I also shared in group.

I am starting to think about some of the jobs I want to do as an adult. I am thinking I would like to be a social worker, or a teen councilor. I am also considering being a fitness instructor, or coming back to Spring Creek Lodge to work with the kids here.'

'March 3*rd*, 1999

Dear Journal,

Going through all this, I have found that I don't like to be taken care of by other people, and I need to be strong. I don't like having to rely on others. I am afraid when I go home I won't fit in anymore.'

'March 4ᵗʰ, 1999

Dead God,

I don't understand some of the things you do sometimes. I am really starting to hate you, and I hate how you let me hate myself. I am never adequate enough, and so far I haven't gotten anywhere in this program without being the exception. Whatever I do is never enough. No one ever sees the changes I make and it's so frustrating. I hate how you made my life and I wish that I never existed. It feels like I don't exist anyways. Why did you give me such a horrible father? Why couldn't you have made him anyone else's Dad? What is so wrong with me? Why did you have to make me so weird? I want to die. I've given up. You're an asshole God. When does the pain ever go away?'

This brings me into my last and final letter I received from my father while in the program. It was obvious that things were always bittersweet with my father. While in the Montana program, several days before I graduated and left, I went through a process they called 'Trail of Lights.' This was unique, as this was the only facility that did this with kids. Trail of Lights was essentially a trust process. Kids were guided through the forest and performed several tasks while blindfolded. Each kid going through the process had their own non-blindfolded buddy who helped them to go through the obstacles. The parents were asked to prepare and send a letter for their children whom were going through the process. The letters were to be sent to the child's case manager, who would give it to the Trail of Lights orchestrator, who would then give the child the letter after completing the event process. It was meant to be a letter praising the strengths of the child, and reflecting on good memories the child and parent shared together.

This is the Trail of Lights letter I received from him:

'*April 11th, 1999*

I remember going to the park with you often. We'd walk down to your school yard and play on big tires, on the swings, on the monkey bars to the very top. I'd climb through the culverts with you. There was a rowboat in the school yard. I remember climbing up with you on the monkey bars to the very top, then holding you up on my shoulders. You were excited, happy, not scared at all. When you got a little radio remote control car, we took it to the schoolyard after hours, and you used it to chase a dog, who wasn't sure what it was. You used to love for me to push the tire swing as hard as I could, sometimes practically over the top! We did the same thing at Temescal Park, and probably went to every park in the area.

Often we'd drive to Montclair Park in the village. There was a mockup old western town structure for kids to play on, and the big kids would climb on top of the town on the roof. You got me to give you a boost so you could play up there, too. At first I would climb up with you, but after a while I just let you go by yourself.

I remember you at about four years old helping me to put together your little red bike. I scrounged a pretty red bicycle for you, but the tires were worn out. I got you a pair of wheels that had new tires on them and you helped me put them on the red bicycle. I showed you how, and you operated the wrench and put on the wheels. Unfortunately, one of the wheels didn't fit, so we took the tire down to the kitchen, heated it in water on the stove, and I took it off one wheel and then the other. Then you put the wheel back on the bike and wanted to go to the park, right away, to learn to ride!

So we did. I put the bike in the little green truck, and we went to the park in the grassy field. I thought the grass would be better because the ground would be softer if you fell. I pushed you all over to help you learn to ride. Later I realized it would have been easier to pedal on asphalt or concrete. I think that was the bike that was in the truck when it was stolen. We kept it there, so we could just go to the park on a whim. I think you were more upset about the bike than about the truck when it was stolen. I got the truck back with hundreds of dollars' worth of damage, but the bike was gone.

Remember when we were in the green truck and spotted a really beautiful rainbow? We drove all over trying to find the pot of gold at the end of it!

I remember you coming home from the pound with a cute little kitten, and you promised you would take care of her (but didn't).

When we moved to Livermore, I remember telling you that you couldn't use a bike for a week because you hadn't come home from school on time. I put the bike in the garage, and locked the front wheel in the trunk of my car. I remember you got into the garage, found the wheel, put it back on the bike, and rode away anyway! I guess figuring out how to do it was a snap at that age. Being obedient or even respectful wasn't your style then. So I took the whole bike to work, and chained it to a post.

Love, Dad'

The letter starts off well. I believe he did have good intentions. However, the last portion of the letter isn't exactly complimentary. Perhaps he saying that I figured out how to get my bike back together was his way of saying that I was intelligent and clever. I have to look pretty hard into it.

I think there are a lot of good metaphors in that letter regarding parenthood, and children learning things for themselves. Sometimes, what the parent thinks is the right way isn't what is best, or what works. Interfering in the path of the child learning for themselves is a fine line. Sometimes a child needs to fall on the asphalt and skin their knees in order to learn how to ride their bike.

There is a difference between trying to prevent a child from falling on the asphalt and preventing them from getting hit by a car in the street. I was a kid who was unhappy, suicidal, and angry. I found myself in trouble with the law a time or two. I smoked cigarettes, and pot, and tried alcohol on a handful of occasions. My grades slipped, and I eventually stopped going to most of my classes because of my social anxiety in a rather rough school. I started hanging out in bad parts of Oakland, and it was likely just a matter of time before I found myself in serious trouble.

I agree that I needed to be removed from the situation I was in. However, I don't know that the measures my father went to were the most responsible choices for me. Perhaps he should have tried having me stay with my Aunt and Uncle first. If things still didn't change it might had been a better idea to send me to a program for teens that was local, where laws existed that protected children. I strongly believe this industry needs to be regulated federally. I might have had a change for the better in a program that lasted under six months where the whole family was able to be actively involved. Perhaps with staff that was qualified to work with children and a licensed therapist.

I can't go back and change the past. All I can do is move on with my life, and count my blessings. It is easier said than done though.

10 – HOME AGAIN

'I think about dying sometimes, but I don't know what that will solve other than my own inner-war and pain. What is paining me so much? What do I not have? What am I missing?'

'April 25th, 1999

Dear Journal,

I am home now from the program. I started school, but I don't fit in. I am so structured I can't stand it. I am having a hard time adjusting. My grandmother has been reading my mail before I get it. My father is trying to seclude me from the rest of the world. He decided to come with me shopping when I got to see his ex-fiancé Callie, because he was afraid she might be trying to manipulate me. He drives me crazy. I need to call my mom.'

'June 5th, 1999

Dear Journal,

I am not living with my Dad anymore; I am living with my mom. I became so upset living with my father that I gathered my belongings and made my way to a pay phone down the street from his house. I made a call to the phone operator asking about places for homeless kids to live. They connected me to my mother over the phone free of charge. I told her that if she didn't take me to live with her, that I was going to run away rather than live with my father any longer. I was afraid if my father found me after I left that he would send me back to the program. My mother came right away and picked me up. Living with my mother is much more normal and less stressful. I have been looking for a job but haven't been able to find one yet.'

'August 5th, 1999

Dear Journal,

I got a job working at a coffee shop. Something about me feels off though since being home. I feel like something bad is going to happen to me, or like something is left undone. I feel sad for some reason, and stressed. I've been feeling bad ever since I went to that group meeting for program parents and program graduates. I've just felt horrible and inadequate. It made me feel as if I had to defend myself. I left feeling inadequate, and like everyone was better than me. I don't feel like anyone is there for me right now. I feel alone. I don't feel close to anyone anymore.'

'November 26th, 1999

Dear Journal,

I made some new friends at work. They are into partying. I tried getting into a rave with them in downtown Oakland, but I wasn't able to get in the door because I am not 18 years old yet.'

'December 6th, 1999

Dear Journal,

I think about dying sometimes, but I don't know what that will solve other than my own inner-war and pain. What is paining me so much? What do I not have? What am I missing? Something doesn't feel complete and I don't understand what it is. I feel like I am searching to have something, or be something, or do something but I don't know what.'

'January 15ᵗʰ, 2000

Dear Journal,

I've really begun to lose faith in God. I feel like people have turned their back on me. I feel so betrayed and alone. No one cares about me. I have been sober for so long, but now I'm starting to believe I should get high. I am thinking of smoking pot again. I used to think that I would be letting down my mother if I started using drugs again. However, right now it's about mending the pain and filling the hole. I feel like there is such a gap in me. I feel like I want to die. I don't understand why I was brought into existence. I'm useless. I feel so alone and empty. I want someone to tell me it's all going to be okay. I don't know how to live an enjoyable life sober. I see myself on the verge of another type of living. Raves and drugs. God, please forgive me for my future mistakes. I need comfort. I feel betrayed.'

'February 22ⁿᵈ, 2000

Dear Journal,

I have been on vacation from work the past two weeks. I've had a lot of fun. I went to a rave and smoked pot a few times. I have been making some new friends.'

'June 23ʳᵈ, 2000

Dear Journal,

I have been so angry about so many things that I can't control. Where did I lose myself in all of this? I used to be able to be a warm person and I cannot even pretend to be that way now. I believe I don't deserve to be happy. I feel like I have really gone off track. I don't understand what I am so angry about. I keep things inside for so long that they won't come out anymore. I feel hostile. Betrayed. I feel let down.'

'August 20ᵗʰ, 2000

Dear Journal,

I have been having panic attacks and insomnia. I feel irritable and inadequate. I don't feel like I can relate to other people. I have been having nightmares frequently about being sent back to Jamaica.'

'September 17th, 2000

Dear Journal,

I don't know how to have relationships with people. I feel so alone, and lonely. I wish I could open up but I can't be vulnerable, and I won't let my walls down. I feel like I am unwanted. I try to look at all the good things I have going on, like going to college, but I have a hard time getting past all these other things that have been overwhelming me.'

11 – GETTING BACK IN TOUCH

'There isn't anyone else in the world who can understand what I went through without actually going through it themselves.'

Getting back into touch with people from the program was difficult at first. It was against the rules to share contact information. The only real likelihood of reuniting with those who were there, at the time I was in the Program, was for the parents to know one another through the parent support groups, and for them to allow their kids to spend time together.

There are a few people in particular whom I was able to keep in touch with immediately following my return home. They have been indispensable people in my life whom I am eternally grateful for. I believe what was left of my sanity at the time was dependent on some of the friendships I made in the program. Without them, I would have felt even more lonely and hopeless than I already did at the time.

Being able to connect with them again was important to me. There isn't anyone else in the world who can understand what I went through without actually going through it themselves. It is kind of like having a war buddy.

Technologies, including the internet and social networking sites have made it much easier to find old friends. The internet was not widely used when I was in the Program. I often wondered for years what happened to one person or another. Being able to chat with them online and being able to see what their lives are like has filled in some gaps. In some ways it was nice to be able to finally connect with people again, and in other ways it's a mixed blessing. The idea of reuniting after so many years is exciting. In other instances though, resentments from interactions in the program have remained through the years.

With the exception of some, I feel better remaining distant from those in the past from the Program. I hate who I was when I was in the program, and I don't like being reminded of it. I was a passive, quiet, timid kid who tried to obey the rules without question and lived in constant anxiety. I wasn't the same person there.

There are a lot of things that stayed with many people from their experience of being in the program. There are many that are still very angry and argumentative. There are those who continue to have paranoia plague them from the fear tactics used in the program. Some still have the maturity level of teenagers. Others have issues with depression, anxiety and nightmares. Nightmares of being sent back is a common theme among those who were in the program, and in many cases is considered part of post-traumatic stress disorder. Other people who attended have issues with addiction, trust issues and have problems that affect their relationships. I think these are all significant consequences from the experience of the program.

There are still people who attended the program and support it. It is concerning to me. I think those might be the ones whom were most affected by the experience. There are plenty of people in the world who justify their abusers. Some try to forget the bad things that happened in the program, and focus just on some of the positive things they gained. They have the right to do so. However, in my opinion, the ends never justify the means.

12 – IN RETROSPECT

'Sometimes bad things do happen to good people.'

The program failed to teach the students realistic tools they could use in their lives. They made an attempt at giving the students a new perception of themselves to strive to be. However, I believe the students were simply too young to really comprehend the material in a useful way. Childhood is meant to prepare for adulthood. Adulthood is where people are meant to figure out who they are and what they are about.

I've turned out pretty well-adjusted and balanced as an adult. However, I've had to work through many issues because of my stay in the program. I believe I lack trust in people as a whole, and because of that I have a hard time asking people for help. I still suffer from anxiety because of the fear-tactics used in the program and the abuse I experienced in my home life. For many years I felt as though I were lying by omission if I withheld any information about myself to other people. The program taught its students this. I've since learned that privacy is not only acceptable, but important.

Some kids were sent to the program because their parents wanted to change the sexual orientation of their child. Their parents did not want to accept them as gay or lesbian, etc. I can only imagine the issues caused by those who went through that.

In the program, my whole life was controlled by other people. As a young adult, I sought control of situations and people in order to try and prevent bad things from happening to me again. Since recognizing this, I have made an effort to change my ways, but it has proven difficult.

Because I was essentially abandoned by my family for two years of my life while in the program, when people would leave my life as an adult it was especially difficult for me. It was more of a challenge for me to deal with when I didn't understand where those feelings stemmed from.

Being sent to the program has greatly affected my relationship with my family. I still hold anger towards my father and grandmother for sending me away, and resentment towards my mother for not finding a way to save me. My fathers' side of the family still believes they did the right thing for me, despite the things I have mentioned to them about my experience. They largely still regard me being sent away because I was a problematic kid, rather than taking responsibility for their part in the chaotic environment they raised me in. It has become a dividing line. I rarely speak to them.

I have found myself in general to be an overly responsible adult, I believe in response to the lack of care I received while in WWASP. I had a stable and successful career in responsible roles for over a decade. I have a difficult time trusting other people to handle things for me properly because of the neglect I experienced in Jamaica. As an adult I have always felt I am ultimately the only person I can depend on. Depending solely on myself worked out up to my late twenties, when I became disabled with chronic pain. And once again, I found I ultimately could not rely on the majority of my family. I used to get worked up over their dysfunction, but have come to realize they are not ever going to change. It has been better for me to keep myself out of their dynamics.

Suffering from chronic pain has forced me to take a serious look at my life. I have come to realize that my experience at WWASP has adversely affected my life in more ways than I had initially thought. I have developed chronic tension of which affects some of my nerves and takes a part in causing pain. Chronic tension has been an effort to suppress anxiety. I have come to learn that total health really does have a mind-body connection. I went on for years suppressing and ignoring things that took a toll on me. I didn't believe that my feelings really mattered because I had become conditioned in WWASP to not be oppositional. I took on things for years believing I was ultimately responsible for everything that happened to me. It made me a tense and critical person and affected my relationships. It took me into my late twenties to change the way I was living my life. At some point I came to truly understand that sometimes bad things do happen to good people. I can't control and be responsible for everything.

With that realization I started to become a much happier person. My life is far from perfect but I am blessed with a lot of great things. I have great people in my life now. I am actually happy. I think being in WWASP helped me to learn how to work towards a goal despite the hardships that can come up along the way. I think that is an important lesson to learn. However, it took me being ill to realize that some hardships are things I elected to put up with and weren't necessary. There is only so far a person should be pushed.

I have had a difficult time transitioning from being a young working professional to being a young person with chronic illness. I have pushed myself to try to continue on even though I probably should had been resting instead. There was a saying that was taught in the WWASP 'TASK' seminars that stuck with me. 'Doing the same thing over and over again expecting different results is the definition of insanity.' It is hard for me to truly embrace the idea of having anything good to take away from WWASP. That saying though is something I won't ever forget. While I think it is my experience at WWASP that made me push myself too hard relentlessly through difficult times, I think it is also WWASP that got me to stop and take a step back. I have come to better accept the physical limitations my chronic pain causes, and have been trying to work with the circumstances that have been dealt to me. My life is slower than it used to be, and it has more meaning. And I am happier. I know what my values are. I don't take on more than I can chew.

I believe my father taking me out of the environment I was in as a teenager was a good choice. It was likely a matter of time until I got into more serious trouble. However, I think sending me to live with other family members might have been a better alternative. Also, I believe I could have benefited from a program with caregivers whom were appropriately trained and qualified to work with children.

Comment []:

I think one of the biggest failures regarding the troubled teen industry is the lack of government regulations. Children's rights are not being appropriately protected until regulations come into place. I think despite earnest efforts of several activist groups to establish basic laws regarding the troubled teen industry, few laws have been established because the owners of these private organizations contribute actively to politicians campaigns. The troubled teen industry is a very profitable business.

I don't have an exact answer as to how to fix the problems in the troubled teen industry. I don't think there is a simple answer. I think having resources available to struggling families is essential. We need to prevent children from being sent to these sorts of places. I think people sharing their personal experiences of facilities for troubled teens is very important. It helps to raise awareness. That is why I have chosen to share my story. Knowledge is power. As my teenaged self once wrote, 'Your will is your power. Don't pretend you don't have it or you won't.'

ABOUT THE AUTHOR

Cindy Art grew up in Northern California. From April 14th 1997- April 14th 1999 she stayed in the WWASP Program as a 'student.' Eighteen months were spent in their Tranquility Bay Program located in Jamaica. An additional six months were spent in WWASP's Spring Creek Lodge Program located in Montana.

5184010R00056

Made in the USA
San Bernardino, CA
29 October 2013